W9-BWP-648

WITHDRAWN
University Libraries
University of Memphis

The study of
ARCHITECTURAL HISTORY

Some other books by Bruce Allsopp

A General History of Architecture
A History of Renaissance Architecture
A History of Classical Architecture
Decoration and Furniture
Historic Architecture of Newcastle upon Tyne
The Great Tradition of Western Architecture
   (*In collaboration with H. W. Booton and Ursula Clark*)
Art and the Nature of Architecture
Style in the Visual Arts
The Future of the Arts
Architecture
Civilization – the next stage

ORIEL GUIDES
   (*In collaboration with Ursula Clark*)
Architecture of France
Architecture of Italy
Architecture of England

The Study of
ARCHITECTURAL
HISTORY

Bruce Allsopp

PRAEGER

BOOKS THAT MATTER

Published in the United States of America in 1970
by Praeger Publishers, Inc.
111 Fourth Avenue, New York, N.Y. 10003

© *1970, in Great Britain, by November Books Limited, London, England*

All rights reserved

Library of Congress Catalog Card Number: 74-129103

Printed in Great Britain

Produced by November Books Limited
Designed by Tom Carter
House Editor: Celia Phillips

Contents

Copy 2

NA
200
A46
1970
cop. 2

Preface and Acknowledgements

In the original lectures a series of slides formed the background to the argument and when they were published in the Journal of the Royal Society of Arts a small selection of illustrations was included in the text. The essence of the book, as it now stands, is the argument, but we are discussing an art which is visually appreciated and my publishers have felt that the text should be accompanied throughout by illustrations. The relationship, however, of the text and illustrations has somewhat changed in translation to book-form and I see the pictures, with their captions, as a running commentary and allusion to the text which, in itself, is a complete argument. Every writer must at times envy the power of a musical composer to write in fugal form, where the parts can intertwine without becoming entangled, but when the writer attempts to do this confusion inevitably results, and the method used here, of text and illustrations in parallel, has allowed me in the captions to deal with some points which could not conveniently be brought into the text without breaking the flow of the argument.

This is not a history of architecture; it is a consideration of the way architecture has been studied historically. The first part is closely based upon the inaugural series of Bossom Lectures which I was invited to deliver at the Royal Society of Arts in 1968 and I am grateful for permission to use this material. It has been somewhat modified in the light of two years of growing older and experiencing a little more of history. The second part is a considerable extension of the closing section of the Bossom Lectures and I am indebted to those who took part in the discussion following the lectures, particularly Mr R. J. Mainstone and Mr S. E. Rigold.

I have also had the privilege of discussing with Mr John Gloag his forthcoming book *The Architectural Interpretation Of History*, and I am grateful for the skilful and sympathetic editorial collaboration of Miss Celia Phillips.

BRUCE ALLSOPP

Architecture, which Michelangelo called the greatest of all the arts, is certainly the one that most faithfully reproduces a people's attitude towards life. It is not history alone but character that is written in buildings. They are the expression of an intellectual and spiritual point of view; they measure the quality of a civilisation, just as surely as they reveal the taste and aptitude of the period to which they belong.

ALFRED, LORD BOSSOM

Part One

The Relationship between Architectural History and Practice

Left
Great Mosque at Córdoba, Spain.

Vernacular architecture in Canterbury, England, the Georgian and the medieval, each representative of its age.

I

During the last half-century great alterations have taken place in both architecture and history. Not only has the modern movement transformed the practice of architecture from a heavy reliance upon historical precedents to a possibly even more lop-sided reverence for technology and finance, but the study of architectural history, and indeed of history as such, has undergone great changes. Its philosophy, as exemplified in the practice of most modern historical scholars, is very different from the 19th-century way of studying history. The nature of the differences in historiography will be dealt with more properly in Part Two, but the consequences should be indicated now because they form the justification for my consideration of the relationship which may exist between history and the practice of architecture.

Briefly, the study of architectural history has never been so ardently and professionally undertaken, as it now is by architectural historians, and at the same time the history of architecture is perhaps less studied by students of architecture than at any time since the Renaissance. We have the paradox of professional architects and town planners who know far less about the history of architecture than many laymen, and I suspect that the main reason for the neglect of history in some of our schools of architecture and town planning is that so many modern architects are only dimly aware that history has changed, that it can be and is very different from what they learned by studying Sir Banister Fletcher's admirable, but in some ways remarkably misleading, book.[1] We also need to consider the very urgent problem of the conflict between new building and the preservation of old buildings. Without some deeper understanding of the relationship between past and present the controversy tends to become unreal and preservation is only too likely to be misrepresented as the antithesis of progress.

There has not always been a relationship between architectural history and practice, for the simple, and at first glance, surprising reason that architecture is much older than history. This is a kind of justification for our contemporaries who reject the study of history; but it does seem to make them culturally cœval with the ancient Egyptians and those laborious anecstors of our own who built Stonehenge!

The history of Egyptian architecture, as we now see it through modern historical spectacles, is particularly interesting because it shows what happened when architecture existed without historical awareness. Egyptian architecture endured for over 3000 years, without undergoing changes sufficiently large to make a significant difference in character and æsthetic, comparable with the change from Roman to Romanesque, or Gothic to Renaissance. In the 2000 years since Cleopatra and the absorption of Egypt into the Roman Empire, there have been, even in Egypt, changes in architecture far greater than in the whole span of ancient Egyptian architecture over three millennia. The reasons lie partly, of course, in the quickening pace of change in civilised communities, but this itself may owe something to the Greek invention of history.

Architecture without history has the unchanging quality of a craft tradition, as

Inverkeithing, Scotland: Market Cross and Sundial, 1688.

Salisbury Plain, England: Stonehenge, c. B.C. *1500.*

when the old cartwright would say, 'That was the way my dad made a cart and my grandad before him and that's the right way to make a cart.' At the risk of enormous oversimplification, there is the essence of ancient architecture, and history appears on the scene, not as a fetter to the past but as a way of escaping from it.

Near Bari, Italy: a trulle, vernacular architecture based on corbel dome construction.

Vernacular architecture, implements and transport at Mondovi, Italy.

Whatever Hesiod may say about Clio, the muse of history, being the daughter of Zeus and Mnemosyne (that is to say, the result of the marriage of supreme divinity with memory), history as we understand it was certainly fathered by Herodotus. Before him there was narrative poetry and what we would now call 'source material'. Though modern research has revealed more truth in Homer than had been suspected, he was certainly no historian. Sagas, epics and chronicles lack the essential quality of history in that they are uncritical. With Herodotus the technique of the Athenian law court was adapted to test the evidence of past events. Where the evidence of witnesses could be sifted, Herodotus seems to be a much better historian than when he had to rely on tradition, on second-hand memories, but his achievement was enormous, and if, to the modern reader, he seems over-credulous about the past, this is because historians have learned, in the last 2500 years, to extend the technique he invented back into the fields of documentation and archæological evidence.

The word 'history' is Greek and means an investigation, an inquiry to find out the truth. As Croiset wrote, Herodotus 'marks a literary revolution'[2] in using it as the title of his work. Collingwood, in *The Idea of History*, said the distinction between Herodotus and a writer of legends is that the historian 'begins by asking questions, whereas the writer of legends begins by knowing something and tells what he knows'.[3] Into this latter category come, I fear, a number of people who have written about architecture under a specious cloak of history. This is part of our present problem.

History seeks to find out the truth, and its method is rational examination of evidence. It is thus scientific. It is also humanistic in that it is about man and his doings. (We use the word 'history' analogously in speaking of the history of the rocks.) It is, in modern jargon, *open-ended*, because it uses the past to illustrate the present and therefore to affect the future. It reveals man to himself and frees him from terrifying isolation in the present. Once man started to think historically, to see himself as part of a process or progression, he had changed his nature significantly and this is reflected in architecture with rather surprising clarity.

Herodotus died in 425 B.C. The old architecture culminated in the Parthenon which had been finished in 432 B.C. The Erechtheum was probably started in 421 B.C. This building is often taken, by those who favour the biological analogy in art history, as the beginning of the decline. I suggest that its significance is really very different and that the Erechtheum symbolises in architecture the point at which tradition and precedent ceased to be binding. One is only a little uneasy that the coincidence of dates is so very close and architecture appears almost incredibly sensitive as a barometer of historical consciousness, of change in man's attitude to the past.

About the quality of the Erechtheum as architecture, I venture to disagree with the eminent authority who called it 'an unsatisfactory building'. I prefer to see it from the point of view of an architect faced with the problem of putting a building alongside the Parthenon, which was still only 10 years old. To have designed a mini-Parthenon in the Doric order would have been trite indeed, and I suggest that this juxtaposition of the small, exquisite, assymetrical, highly-ornamented Ionic shrine to the ponderous, dignified, austere mass of the Parthenon is one of the most successful relationships of two buildings which

Athens, Greece: the Parthenon and the Erechtheum.

has ever been achieved. Furthermore, there is nothing final about the Erechtheum. Despite the extreme refinement of its detail it is a mutation, the beginning of a new architecture capable of all the variations which Hellenistic, Roman, Medieval and Renaissance architects were to be able to invent. The Parthenon was an end and it could only have come about at the end of a tradition. It was thus described by Fergusson:

For intellectual beauty, for perfection of proportion, for beauty of detail, and for the exquisite perception of the highest and most recondite principles of art ever applied to architecture, it stands utterly and entirely alone and unrivalled – the glory of Greece and a reproach to the rest of the world.[4]

But before we accept the validity of this reproof we ought to consider the price that was paid for it in the inhibition of experiment and originality and of the ability of society to adapt itself. The Parthenon stands, not for the achievements of Socrates but for those elements in Greek society which destroyed him, and perhaps even for his noble obstinacy in insisting upon his own death as a logical conclusion.

Every architectural element in the Parthenon, except the stylobate of stone, faithfully interprets forms invented for timber, and behind the timber forms there are the sanctities of sacred groves, of sacral trees and pillars and subliminal symbolism. The practice of architecture was extended from a holy rite and retained a ritual character. For this there is documentary evidence in Vitruvius. It is this religious element which raises ancient Greek architecture above the level of a craft. It is not merely that trial and error have produced the best solution which is then handed on from father to son like the cartwright's trade mentioned above. From the earliest times more than functional efficiency was required from the architect. It was understood that his was a holy art, a mystery governed by strict rules of practice which were not to be logically examined or historically considered. Like the blind story-teller who spoke the legends which he knew to be true, the architect practised according to laws which he knew to be right, laws like the grammar of the language he spoke and of which no man knew the origin.

Even in the materialistic Roman age, when the worship of nature in divine personifications had degenerated into crude and often brutal superstition, Vitruvius persists in the ancient attitude to his art. He does not argue, and though he cites authorities in a way which is quite surprising, if we consider it historiographically in the context of its period, he does so because they express with more authority than he can himself as a Roman architect, the true and ancient doctrine. This attitude comes through into his teaching of practical matters. 'The length of dining rooms must be twice their width,' he says, in the same dogmatic way as he rules that 'if the bases are to be Ionic their proportions are to be so fixed that the breadth of the base each way is one and three eighths of the thickness of a column'. It seems that it will take more than 20 centuries to free ourselves of this ritualistic dogmatism in architecture, for where religion moves out technology moves in with new orthodoxies.

Vitruvius had the wisdom of the practical man. He had great respect for learning without himself being a scholar. He stated once and for all the basic problem of architectural education in the first sentence of *De Architectura*.[5] 'The skill of the architect is furnished from many disciplines and various studies derived from other arts' He was the archetypal architect, empirical, highly intelligent and wide-ranging in his ideas, but also credulous, dogmatic and yearning for recognition in the practice of an art where censure is more commonly awarded than praise, especially by fellow architects! It is mainly through Vitruvius in his largely unacknowledged role of a historian, that we know about the impact of Greek philosophy and science upon architecture. This had happened after the building of the Parthenon, and its effect was partly to replace the religious mystical element in architecture by a scientific and philosophical mystique.

The contribution of Greek science to architecture was not technological. It did not facilitate construction or improve environment, but it did provide an absolute foundation for the theory of design by relating architecture to the scientist's concept of an ordered world constructed out of elements which all bore a due proportional relationship to each other. One may speculate about how near the Greeks came to understanding the structure of matter but their atomic theory was imprisoned by their assumptions. Their manner of *a priori* reasoning was the insuperable obstacle which had to be pushed right away before modern science could begin. By 'scientific' I mean Greek-scientific and would stress, as must be emphasised again in discussing the early Renaissance, that architectural theory was clearly based upon science as then understood, upon the best science of the age. I doubt if we ourselves could justly say the same about modern architecture and I do not want, at this stage, to discuss the details of classical architectural theory which was to receive its finest expression 2000 years later in the writing of Leon Battista Alberti.

Reverting to the Parthenon, that criterion of architectural excellence, we may say that in the period before Herodotus architects practised within an essentially backward-looking æsthetic. It is impossible for talented artists to work without making *some* contribution of their own, but the milieu in which Greek designers worked, up to the end of the 5th century, was such as to reduce change to a minimum. They worked under the ægis of the past, not in the light of history.

With the birth of historical thinking the pace of change quickened and the scope for originality increased. This may be more a coincidence than a cause-and-effect relationship, and it might be true to say that the climate which produced Herodotus, the same moving spirit of the age (if we may admit that such a phenomenon can exist), was made manifest in the arts, in politics, in the disaster of the Peloponnesian war, in the career of Alexander the Great.

From the 4th century onwards the architect's role was less arcane and more like modern practice. The old orders were handled with greater freedom and the faults of the Doric order were criticised. This we know from Vitruvius. The new order, the Corinthian, was the first to be designed rather than evolved. And it was in the so-called Hellenistic period that the principles and proportions of the orders of architecture were consolidated in the form in which they were to be handed on through Rome to the Renaissance. For the modern historian of architecture, if he is at all conditioned by the Greek Revival – and it is difficult not to be – it is necessary to make an effort to recapture the Renaissance vision of classical architecture as a way of design rooted in Hellenistic Greece, in Syracuse,

Nîmes, France: the Maison Carrée. The Roman continuation of the Greek tradition.

Pergamon, Ephesus and Alexandria as well as Corinth and Athens, and culminating in the architecture of Imperial Rome.

The form in which Vitruvius wrote *De Architectura*, so to speak, on the evening before Roman architecture burst into flower, gives a fascinating picture of the dichotomy of architectural thinking in the Roman period. In theory he relies upon the teaching of Hellenistic writers such as Hermogenes and he is a typical Roman in accepting the Greeks as his masters in cultural and artistic matters, but the other, and larger, part of his book is practical and rooted in contemporary experience. He chooses a site for its healthiness, a timber for its resistance to fire and explains the best methods of water supply. In this he is true to his terms of reference, stated in Book One, the mastery both of technical skill and æsthetic theory, both of which are necessary to the accomplished architect.

What does not appear in Vitruvius, because he wrote fifty years too early, is the architectural dilemma posed by the great advances in Roman structural design, the use of concrete, of cross vaults and of domes. These were never fully integrated into a Roman system of architecture because Roman piety towards tradition made the acceptance of a new architecture impossible. The façade of the Colosseum, with its post and lintel orders superimposed upon the structure of arches and vaults, tells us a great deal about the unhistorical attitude of the Romans towards the past. They remained prisoners of traditional authority, prisoners in a legendary stage of thinking about the past. Vitruvius sees the past

Above: Rome, Italy: the Colosseum.
Below: Volterra, Italy: the reputedly-Etruscan city gateway.

in terms of authority and the present in terms of practicality. The historical concept of process, of transition, would have been able to resolve this tension because it would have shown the past as, equally with the present, a process and not a crystallisation.

Oddly enough, the Romans were capable of an historical attitude towards the future. They took over the Egyptian and Etruscan idea of monumentality – and here I use the word in its proper sense of a sepulchre, a reminder of the dead – and they secularised it. The living built monuments to themselves in the form of gateways, markets, fora and other civic embellishments with an idea of enhancing their status while alive and with an eye to their reputation with posterity. So the legendary æsthetic of the past is harnessed to the technology of the present with a view to history in the future. And it must be admitted that the historian in the present day has reason to be thankful for this far-sighted if sometimes rather conceited sense of the *future* of history.

Until the time of Constantine, Roman architecture was the vesture of the Roman state, as much a part of it as the Latin language. It was capable of great invention and originality of structural and spatial conception, as in the Thermae of Caracalla, but this had to be confined within a web of the antiquated but venerable and beautiful architectural forms.

The Edict of Milan in A.D. 313 and the transfer of the administration to Constantinople in A.D. 330 initiated a short but brilliant period of creativity in the Middle East. Its historical interest for us lies not only in the development of a new system of structural design but also in the exemplar of what can happen to a modern movement in architecture when it becomes subject to an efficiently regnant bureaucracy. The creative phase of Byzantine art was contained in two centuries.

In Banister Fletcher, social and historical considerations precede each of the periods chosen by him for what he called 'study on the comparative method'. I doubt if many architects have given much attention to these social and historical notes, and I think they may be excused for any such neglect because those sections are so abbreviated as to be inevitably dogmatic and often distorted into wrongness by the forces of compression, but Sir Banister's idea was good in that it recognised the consequential nature of architectural history.

Architecture is the art and science of building man's environment and inevitably there is a dialogue between what man wants and what architects can do, as also between what the architect can conceive and what men will accept and pay for. The architect-client partnership is an indissoluble bond in a sense that marriage is not. For no matter how firmly one may believe that marriages are made in heaven, there is the possibility of being single. The architect, however, cannot function without a client unless he pays for the building himself. No matter how strong an ivory tower the architect may construct, the client end of the partnership is bound to be conditioned by the laws, customs, exigencies, economics, prejudices, follies, politics and fortunes of the society in which he lives, and one of the uses of history is to employ the past as a laboratory where demonstrations of social and political causes and effects can be studied.

The Byzantine period is obviously of interest in this way as an indication of the possible course of architectural history and practice in any matured bureaucracy such as our own. It is easy to see the danger of a brave modern movement

Benevento, Italy: the Arch of Trajan, showing the combination of the Roman structural arch with the Greek post and lintel structural system used as decoration.

Right
The royal monogram, 1968, on architecture of the utmost mediocrity, at Durham, England.

degenerating into dull conformity with Ministry regulations and optima devised by accountants. It has happened before.

The Banister Fletcher system of comparative study foundered most heavily on what was isolated as the 'Early Christian Period', the age of transition from classical to medieval architecture. The name 'barbarian' has been overloaded with woadish connotations and the evolution of Romanesque architecture in the so-called 'Dark Ages' has been misrepresented by most architectural historians (Lethaby was a notable exception) because the social component in the architectural history of the 4th to 9th centuries far outweighs the stylistic component. There is also the fact that the perishable nature of architecture in wood, and the fire-raising propensities of the Northmen, have eliminated most of the built evidence.

But architectural history does not stop because the Northmen liked architectural bonfires. To some extent it goes underground and can be recovered by excavating post-holes, but the absurdity of there being gaps in architectural history points to a flaw in our concept of what architectural history is and how it should be studied. In some ways those periods which have left us little in

Tournai Market Place and Cathedral. A city which has a strong sense of the value of its past. Here the earliest kings of France were crowned.

remains are the most interesting. We ourselves in the 1970s, if we care about what our own history will look like to posterity, certainly have an interest in discouraging the conclusion, which might be drawn from many histories of architecture, that palaces, temples and churches are all that really matter.

We know that in the 4th and 5th centuries Roman architecture flourished on such a scale in the west that Trier had two thermal establishments as grand as the Thermæ of Caracalla and the Thermæ of Diocletian in Rome, as well as a double basilica, half of which was converted into a large medieval cathedral. The architecture was Roman. In the late 8th century at Aachen something very like S. Vitale at Ravenna was being built. But in the 11th century there was a new kind of architecture based on the Roman, but quite different in character, much more free, expressive in its sculptural detailing, exciting in its structural inventiveness. The *process* by which this change came about is of profound interest and by no means so obscure as we have been led to believe, provided that we see architectural history as part of the history of man; provided that, in other words, we remember the importance of the client as well as the artifacts of the architects.

How we might study the history of architecture between the 5th and 11th centuries can be only slightly indicated here. We should not be much concerned with actual works of architecture because they are few and sometimes unrepresentative, as is Aachen cathedral, but as architectural historians we should take into account the barbarians' attitude to Rome – generally one of reverence, and even nostalgia, as is indicated by the successive attempts of Gothic kings to re-establish the grandeur of Rome. We should consider the attitudes induced by Christianity, the destruction in Gaul for example, of temples to Mercury and

Poitiers, France: St Jean, a rare survival from the Merovingian period.

their replacement by Christian shrines on the same site, as at Puy de Dôme and Montmartre; the horror felt by Christians at the Mithraic sacrament which seemed a vile parody of the Eucharist; the effects of plague, which were far more terrible than the invasions by barbarians; the consequent impoverishment and shortage of labour indicated, for example, by allocation of large tracts of land round Clermont Ferrand to Saxon prisoners in the 6th century so that the soil might be cultivated again. Then there is the Church, the survival of Latin as the language of culture and the monopoly of learning by ecclesiastics. We should pay more attention to the devastation of the Norse invaders and take a look at such sagas as the Gudrun. We should also bear in mind the oppressive belief in the Day of Judgement being at hand and the widespread conviction, as the year 1000 approached, that this would be the end of architecture and the end of history, the opening of the gates of heaven and hell. It is perhaps salutary for us, in our day, to reflect that the apocalyptic prophecies were a more stulti-fying threat than the possibility that modern man might be so foolish as to start a thermo-nuclear war.

In the dark ages some people were certainly thinking historically. *The History of the Franks*, by St Gregory of Tours,[6] is a by no means negligible work and it

The vaults of St Saturnin in Auvergne, France.

is one of many. But the histories of those times do not admit to any pleasure in the present or confidence in the future. They are backward-looking and so, by and large, must the architecture have been. It looked back at great monuments which were no longer technically possible and yet in contriving to emulate them with inadequate means, to build with small units of hand-wrought stone, it made some progress towards a new architecture.

Perhaps the most striking fact about the history of medieval architecture is the liberation which occurred in the 11th century. Within 100 years, 93 to be exact, the high ribbed vaults of Durham cathedral had been conceived and partly built.

The chancel vaults, Durham Cathedral, England; a breakthrough in architectural technique.

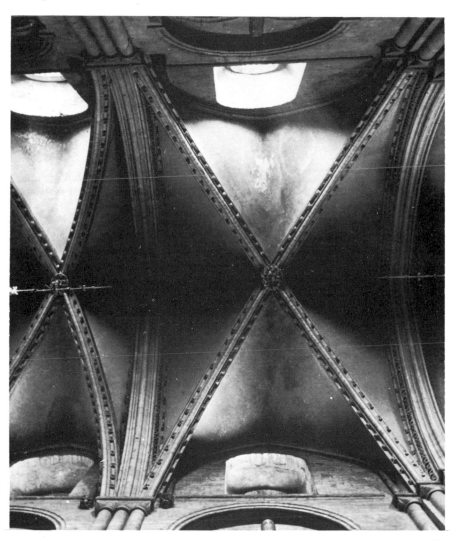

Durham Cathedral, England.

Right
Detail of a capital at Issoire, France. The Romanesque re-interpretation of the Corinthian order in which the repetitive craftsman is replaced by the individual sculptor creating a unique work of art within the limitations of the capital form.

Architecture no longer looked back over its shoulder at the unattainable quality of Roman design. The orders of architecture were now handled with a freedom which is usually mistaken for ignorance, and the art of using structure as a medium for the designing of enclosed space suddenly and dramatically came to life. The reasons for this abrupt enlivenment were undoubtedly complex and the feeling of starting off afresh on a second thousand years was only one of them. Perhaps the two most significant events were the enforcement of celibacy for the priesthood (1074) by Pope Gregory VII and the Norman conquests of northern France, Sicily and England which established security from Scandinavian invasions and raids. The Norse component in western European civilisation had become established and constituted a formidable defence

against further migrations from their original homelands.

Just as English aristocratic ancestry is traced back to 1066, but not beyond, so the historians of western Europe have tended to accept the 11th century as a base-line upon which the nations become consolidated. Thereafter a relatively stable system of government and a social hierarchy based on service – the feudal system – were established. The system worked; the lords of Church and State acquired the resources which have been called the sinews of war and could equally be called the life-blood of architecture, an art which, throughout the ages, has been dependent upon the availability of money to a greater extent than any other art.

The Romanesque period was rightly divided between two volumes in Clapham's famous history of it,[7] but in England the very term Romanesque has been generally abandoned for the later period which is commonly called Norman architecture. On the Continent no such convenient distinction can be made, and

The Abbey Church of Lessay in Normandy, France (restored). Characteristic Romanesque.

the term Romanesque is somewhat misleading when applied to the adventurous structures of Auvergne or Burgundy. These, far from looking back to Rome, are conceived in an æsthetic which is moving rapidly away from Rome, in structure and planning as well as in the vivid, sensitive and individualistic sculpture which not only adorns them but is also an essential part of the architectural concept.

Almost all the basic ideas which contributed to the medieval achievements of the 13th and 14th centuries were in being in the 11th and 12th centuries. That was the creative period when the great decisions were taken. Given the structural and planning invention inherent in Durham and St Saturnin, then Amiens and Wells were a natural development. The invention, or more properly, the introduction, of the pointed arch was certainly a very useful device but it was not the hinge at the joint of history which merely stylistic histories have made it.

It is very tempting to make comparisons between the first 200 years of the second millennium and the modern movement in architecture, but such parallels

Typical Provençal Romanesque church of Le Thor.

are apt to be misleading and I shall firmly resist the lure of comparison between Le Corbusier and the Romanesque. This would be a critical *jeu d'esprit* rather than a serious historical exercise. What I want to ask is how the medieval architect thought of history, and it is by no means easy to answer. One reason is that medieval historians have not asked this question. There might be plenty of evidence if it were looked for in the right places by suitably qualified scholars. This indeed is one of the excitements of history which is obscured from those who have never done research and believe that history is a finite subject. In fact a great many questions remain to be asked and answers to be wrung from the evidence of the past.

It has been suggested that medieval architecture was so good and so 'modern' because medieval architects were not interested in history, and this has even

Autun Cathedral, France: timpanum, by Giselbertus.

been adduced as a good reason for not studying history in our schools of architecture. The facts are quite different and the implication might well be taken as a warning to the architectural profession.

The truth of the matter must be sought in an examination of the medieval way of organising a building contract. It was often supposed in the past, before Knoop and Jones[8] and John Harvey[9] had shown how wrong this was, that medieval cathedrals were designed by bishops and even constructed by dedicated amateurs. Modern scholarship has looked behind the legends and revealed the complex structure of the medieval building industry. Clearly the master mason and the master carpenter were architects in that they were designers of buildings as well as constructors, but there was an element of truth in the old idea. The supervising role of the modern architect, which as we all know has an important effect on design decisions, was taken by the client or his clerk of works, and the clerk of works was of a very different stamp from his modern counterpart, a man of high social and intellectual standing, a scholar such as Geoffrey Chaucer or

Soria, Spain: portal of Santo Domingo.

William of Wykeham, who became, in fact, Bishop of Winchester and Lord High Chancellor of England.

History, albeit somewhat different in character from history as we now understand it, was certainly studied in the Middle Ages and *De Architectura*, by Vitruvius, was carefully copied. Indeed we only know it from medieval texts, of which there are many. Architectural history and theory, it would seem, were largely the study of the patrons, not of the executants, of architecture, a situation which arose again in England in the 18th century. In both periods the status of the architectural 'profession', if one may be permitted so tendentiously to call

33

Laon Cathedral, France: classical form clearly retained in early Gothic design.

Laon Cathedral, France: detail of the western porches, with Roman Corinthian order, elongated to suit the medieval taste.

it that, was lowered, but the architectural result in the quality of buildings was quite excellent.

Let us turn for a moment to the most famous of medieval scholars who thought about beauty, St Thomas Aquinas. His definition was this:

For beauty there are three requirements. First, a certain wholeness or perfection, for whatever is incomplete is, so far, ugly; second, a due proportion or harmony; and third, clarity, so that brightly coloured things are called beautiful.[10]

It is difficult not to recognise this as particularly applicable to architecture and certainly a medieval scholar, in any of the great monastic foundations, who lived and worshipped in the presence of great architecture, could hardly have written about beauty without thinking of nobly proportioned piers and vaults and of spaces transfused by sunlight through coloured windows.

What happened in the middle ages was a workable division of labour whereby the master mason was expert in the technique and craft lore of architecture and, as Villard d'Honnecourt's[11] sketch book shows, made careful studies of modern work by his rivals. There is little if any evidence that he was a man of generalised learning, a man of culture or a scholar. On the other hand the patron, paymaster and to a large extent the controller and organiser of the project was likely to be a man learned in history, philosophy and theology. It was a system which worked and produced magnificent architecture. The miracle it achieved was to elevate the folk art of building to a level where it could be expressive of the loftiest aspirations of the religious, to the state of being a flexible, developing, transcendental and mystical art.

We are back to the polarity of client and architect, the two forces without which architecture cannot happen, and we might pause to consider our present predicament. I suggest it is not at all like that of the medieval architect, and we must now be concerned with the decay of the medieval way of building and the emergence of quite a new kind of architect. The relationship of architect and client, and the relationship of each to history, became completely different.

II

I have tried to show how the birth of history in the work of Herodotus was linked with a change in the practice of architecture, a change symbolised in the different qualities of the Parthenon and the Erechtheum. Awareness of something called history freed architects from the dogma of the past, partially disentangled the mysteries of their art from the obfuscations of antique religion and made possible, in the Hellenistic age, the development of a body of æsthetic theory rooted in philosophy and science as then understood. This science involved an

Florence, Italy: Santa Maria del Fiore.

overall concept of the rational unity of the world and the belief that it was built up out of modules in such a way that all the parts were whole-number multiples of the basic unit. This modular concept of the world was already reflected in the design of the Parthenon, the basic unit being in that building one half of the diameter of the base of the Doric columns, but the proportional system was applied to a way of design which was backward-looking, inflexible and, for a building in stone, essentially irrational.

The systematised theory of the Hellenistic world comes to us through Vitruvius, who accepted it as dogma and grafted on to it a great deal of practical 'know-how' which ought to be required corrective reading for everyone who thinks that any particular technology is an enduring and elemental component of architecture. Vitruvius recognised that mere building, no matter how excellent, was not architecture if it lacked what Fergusson called, in assessing the Parthenon, 'intellectual beauty'.

36

This idea of intellectual beauty, of architecture as the product of a highly cultivated mind, persisted in the Middle Ages but was given an additional dimension, which was the perfection of structural form. Classical architecture seems to have taken no account of what we should now call structural elegance.

Newcastle upon Tyne, England: the lantern of the Cathedral tower daringly carried on flying buttresses counter-weighted with heavy pinnacles.

The mind of the architect, as Le Corbusier insisted in his commentary on the Parthenon,[12] was concerned with the beauty of pure form. Formal beauty was achieved by applying a strict intellectual discipline of related proportion and optical correction to a given system of construction. The Gothic age did not abandon formal discipline, though the extent to which formal geometry was used is a matter of dispute, but it developed an additional discipline of structural refinement which was a new element in architecture. A strange feature of this is the apparent inability of the medieval architect to calculate structure mathematically; but it should be noted that even the modern engineer has to proceed by way of intuition of a shape first and calculation of its behaviour second. Experience is still a substitute for calculation in many design decisions, and there seems to be such a thing as intuitive mathematics, a subject which deserves more investigation.

On the threshold of the Renaissance we find the Florentine architect, Brunelleschi, solving the problem of building a dome on Sta Maria del Fiore, by just such a process of structural-mathematical intuition. It is a structure which would be extremely difficult to calculate even now. In Brunelleschi's work the two disciplines of form and structural elegance are marvellously balanced. He had a foot in the Middle Ages and the other in the new world of the Renaissance, but his back was to the past and he was stepping forward into the new.

The very word 'Renaissance' suggests history. It means the rebirth of classical civilisation, and when Brunelleschi set off in 1401, with Donatello, to study and measure the ancient architecture of Rome he was closing the door upon the medieval way of design. What he did was to take up the study of history, in a very modern way, by going back to primary sources. It would however be quite wrong to suggest that Brunelleschi started the Renaissance. Architecture is remarkably sensitive to the climate of the time but architects are seldom if ever originators of that climate. They may in fact be conveniently divided into two classes, chameleons and leopards, those who adapt and those who never change their spots. Brunelleschi was definitely in the former category and his Pazzi Chapel has somewhat the same significance as the Erechtheum. History had become of paramount importance in architecture, not merely as an exemplar, for that is not really history at all, but as a technique for recovering what was valuable and had been lost in the æsthetic of architecture and enlivening the present by the quality standards of the past. Once again the study of history coincides with enlightenment and change. This is what we should expect because the study of history is born of curiosity and desire for the truth. It is fostered by freedom and helps to sustain freedom but under authoritarian governments and in monolithic, change-resistant societies, the occupation of a true historian can be dangerous or impossible.

Brunelleschi studied primary sources, the Roman ruins, and felt the warm wind of humanism which was to bring so many bright flowers into bloom. He interpreted his new knowledge, and the feeling of a new spring-time in the affairs of men, through his architecture. This is the role of the artist. Brunelleschi was not a historian but he was an artist with the feeling for history. The great historian and theorist of the age was Alberti, a man of immense importance in the development of western architecture, and it seems appropriate to digress a little in order to remind ourselves what manner of man he was.

Florence, Italy: the Pazzi Chapel by Brunelleschi.

Leon Battista Alberti was born in 1404 and belonged to one of the great Florentine families in exile. He had a university education and was a young man of outstanding intellectual ability. By hard work, by many different talents, by what Adrian Stokes[13] called 'a sensitive yet robust temper expressed in terms of a broad aristocracy of mind', Alberti achieved for himself the position of an aristocrat without estate, a position in Renaissance society somewhat similar to that of a great artist but subtly different and more influential. Though he practised as an architect this was merely incidental, or at most a contributory incentive, to his great achievement, and it is highly significant that Alberti did

39

not write for architects directly: he wrote in Latin for his intellectual peers. He addressed himself to the scholar and the cultured aristocrat. This was perhaps fortunate and the success of his work tends to confirm a view which we have already taken in this book, namely, that architects do not themselves control the way architecture will go. From the 15th to the 18th century the patrons of architecture almost invariably required the kind of architecture which rested upon the foundation of Alberti's theories, reinterpreted, adapted, edited many times by Palladio, Vignola, Serlio, Scamozzi and others but still, even in the Greek revival and French academic neo-Classicism, essentially Alberti.

Alberti was not an original theorist. He did not try to invent. His attitude to his work was always that of the scholar, to *find* the truth, not to *make* it as the artist may, and his method was historical. The one great assumption in Alberti's *De Re Aedificatoria* is that the ancients had the right answer. In Chapter 1 of Book VI he wrote:

It grieved me that so many great and noble instructions of ancient authors should be lost by the injury of Time, so that scarce any but Vitruvius has escaped this general wreck: a writer indeed of universal knowledge, but so maimed by age, that in many places there are great chasms, and many things imperfect in others. Besides this his style is absolutely void of all ornaments and he wrote in such a manner, that to the Latins he seemed to write Greek, and to the Greeks Latin: but indeed it is plain that . . . he might almost as well have never wrote at all . . . since we cannot understand him.[14]

Faced with this appalling difficulty, which might be compared with reconstructing the dramas of Euripides, if all his works had been lost and only descriptions of them existed, Alberti turned to the ancient philosophers, to Pythagoras and to Plato, to even the slightest references in any of a great number of classical texts and to the actual buildings left by the Romans. But whether he was studying ancient cosmology or the ruins of a Roman temple, Alberti's aim was always the same, to deduce from the surviving evidence what were the *principles* of classical design. Given his one basic assumption that the ancients had the secret system of beauty, then it ought to be possible to work back from an Arch of Trajan or a Temple of Mars to the principles which had been followed in designing it. Book IX of *De Re Aedificatoria*, which states the evidence and the rules deduced from the evidence, is a quite remarkable piece of infinitely painstaking and scrupulous historical research, and though historiographers have taken little notice of it I think it may well be the earliest example of modern historical research.

Like Herodotus, Alberti was too great a man to have any immediate followers. His work was published after his death and translated into Italian in the mid-16th century. As so often happens, the results of his research into principles were applied as rules of thumb by practising architects, and made widely available in Palladio's *Four Books of Architecture*.[15]

Up to the death of Bramante in 1514, and possibly a little longer, the lofty intellectual qualities of Alberti's kind of architecture persisted, but political, religious and social changes, highlighted by the sack of Rome in 1527, discredited the concept of an ordered world and sickened the taste of a corrupt, bewildered society for the calm, dignity and unity of Renaissance design. But the different

Todi, Spain: S. M. della Consolazione. The perfection of High Renaissance design.

character of Mannerist and Baroque architecture should not be allowed to mislead us into believing that the fundamental architectural æsthetic had been lost. Following Alberti architects persisted in geometrical experimentation and explored three-dimensional geometry which Alberti had largely ignored, but instead of their geometry being rooted in the supposed nature of the universe, in science as Alberti had understood it, Mannerist and Baroque architects mistook the slide on the screen for the source of the picture in the projector and experimented with geometry and proportional relationships as such. This process still goes on and the *basic art* which is taught in schools derives from Alberti. The difference is, however, that Alberti, as he said in his book, would have tested his own designs by the rules and found, to his sorrow, how poor was his unaided intuition, whereas the modern artist and critic have no rules grounded in scientific understanding of the nature of things. Science, of course, has advanced a very long way since the 15th century and art has lost touch with it, but the old attitudes persist.

Alberti was a genuine historian, and through him history enlightened architecture. After him the freedom which seems to result from any new enlightenment produced a vast amount of experimentation and achievement in the arts and not least in architecture, but the study of architectural history declined to the quarrying level, where architects looked to the past for useful design ideas, not for understanding of the nature of their art; and I think it is true to say that with the decline of intellectual endeavour the patronage of architecture became more dogmatic.

If we now turn to France and the châteaux of the Loire, we find a strange reversal of the role of history. In the reign of Francis I the Gothic tradition was still very strong and the attitude of the master-mason type of architect was hardened against the introduction of foreign ways. French aristocracy produced no equivalent of the Medici, and Renaissance architecture could not be founded, as in Italy, upon the patronage of an educated aristocracy. Moreover, power was already centralised in the monarchy and was to become more so. Renaissance architecture was to be introduced as a style of design, largely by royal authority, and since the French architects were against it Italians were imported to design in the modern manner. French architects were leopards all, except for the obscure Jules le Breton, who did his best to follow the Latin style without

Fontainebleau: the north side of the Cour du Cheval Blanc by Le Breton.

any understanding of its true nature. History, it seemed, was all against the new fashion and Renaissance architecture had no intellectual roots in French soil. Here is an interesting example of a long rearguard action being fought with the supposed authority of history against the new architecture.

But in saying this are we using the word 'history' in a wrong sense? I do not think so. It was a reasonable interpretation of history to say that Gothic was the architecture of France but past history is no effective barrier against the tides of the present. Though historical *precedent* is often used as an argument against change this appeal to the 'authority' of the past never seems to be effective for long, and in the fluid state of French society in the 16th century, change was inevitable. Human societies do not adjust to new conditions by adhering to precedents but by their modification or rejection, and the 'sense of history' is, as we have already noted, often the means of moving forward, the 'authority' for change. What the French master masons were trying to do, and what all re-actionaries are inclined to do, was to use history to stop history; and since history is properly concerned with truth and not with old dogma it does not work like this.

The spectacle of French medieval-type architects yielding pride of place, as well as kind of architecture, to Italians is interesting and not without relevance to architects who find themselves committed to working in an age of transition, such as our own. The old kind of architect had to go despite all his virtues, his craft lore and his organisation. The Italians submitted to subtle French influences, and Primaticcio's work at Fontainebleau foreshadows the truly French archi-tecture of François Mansart in the 17th century. But among the great names of architects in the 16th and 17th centuries one alone stands out as of crucial importance for our present study; that of Philibert de l'Orme. The reason lies, not in his architecture, though this was of considerable interest, but in his book *L'Architecture* which was published in 1567.[16] De l'Orme follows the pattern of architect-thinkers which had been set by Vitruvius, in that he combines practical technology with theory. The technology reveals him as a man of great ingenuity, but this is now no more than interesting source material for historians of the technique of building. His ideas about the nature of architecture and its relation to history are, however of fundamental importance and they are aptly summar-ised in his own chapter heading:

That it is permitted, by the example of the ancients, to invent and make new columns, and so I have designed some and called them French columns.[17]

Here was the rankest heresy! Here was history used to justify a deviation from classical precedent. If we link with this Philibert's equally outrageous statement that:

It would be much better in my opinion for the architect to fail in the ornamentation of his columns, in the proportion and treatment of façades . . . than that he should desert Nature's excellent rules which concern the comfort, convenience and advantage of the inhabitants, and not the decoration, beauty and richness of houses, made only to please the eye, and not for any benefit to the health and life of men.[18]

43

Par les susdicts moyens vous ne
ferez seulement des colomnes Do-
riques composées de plusieurs pieces, mais aussi des Ioniques, & de
quelque autre ordre que vous vou-
drez : voire à la façon & imitation
des arbres, ainsi que nous auons dit.
Pour doncques vous donner quelque cognoissance de nostre dire, ie
vous ay figuré cy-auprés vne colô-
ne de l'ordre Ionique, laquelle i'a-
uois dressée & faicte expressément
pour estre appliquée au Palays de la
maiesté de la Royne mere: mais, cô-
me le bon vouloir luy a creu de faire sondit Palays fort magnifique, &
beaucoup plus riche qu'elle n'auoit
deliberé au commençement, apres
auoir faict poser les basses & pre-
mieres assiettes des colónes, il m'a
fallu prendre vne autre sorte d'or-
nements & façon trop plus riche:
voire iusques à faire tailler & inscul-
per plusieurs sortes d'ouurages &
deuises (ordonnées par sa maiesté)
sur lesdictes basses & assiettes qui
sont faictes de marbre: ainsi que
vous le pourrez plus amplement
voir & cognoistre par les figures des-
dictes colomnes, lesquelles ie vous
representeray au second Tome &
volume de nostre Architecture, ou
nous descrirons bien au long, Dieu
aydant, ledit Palays. Ce temps pen-
dant vous verrez la figure que ie
propose cy-auprés, pour monstrer
comme lon doit faire de plusieurs
pieces les colomnes Ioniques, &
toutes autres.

R iij

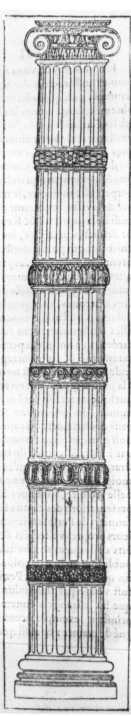

*Colomne de
l'ordre Ioni-
que composée
de plusieurs
pieces, pour le
Palays de la
Royne mere.*

Des portes du dedans des logis, pour entrer aux falles, chambres,
garderoubes, galleries, & autres lieux. (CHAP. XIII.

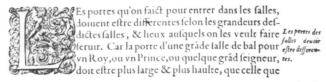

Es portes qu'on faiĉt pour entrer dans les falles,
doiuent eftre differentes felon les grandeurs def-
diĉtes falles, & lieux aufquels on les veult faire *Les portes des*
feruir. Car la porte d'une grãde falle de bal pour *falles deuoir eftre differen-*
vn Roy, ou vn Prince, ou quelque grãd feigneur, *tes.*
doit eftre plus large & plus haulte, que celle que

Design by Philibert de l'Orme for a gateway: from L'Architecture.

Left: An 'Ionic' order designed by Philibert de l'Orme.

we may well consider that Philibert de l'Orme has some claim to be called the
first of the moderns.

Here again history is showing the way ahead and is being used to refute old
dogma.

But Philibert de l'Orme was a very long way ahead of his time, and his attitude
to history and indeed his philosophy of architecture had, so far as I am aware, no
immediate followers and did not affect the main trends of French thought in the
17th century. It is however, interesting to speculate whether the rationalism
of French architects in the 18th century may have owed something to de l'Orme's
precocity. I rather doubt it because this rationalism was reflected in architecture
rather than generated by architects, as nearly always seems to be the case.

Philibert de l'Orme appears to be one of the very rare architects who was in advance of the intellectual climate of his own time.

Having reached the 16th century by way of a fairly clear route from Greece and Rome, through France and England in the Middle Ages and then abruptly back to Italy because of the Renaissance, and so to France whither Italian ideas were transplanted and took firm root, we are now confronted with a parting of the ways so complex that it might almost have been designed by a modern traffic engineer. Being in France I must keep to the right, and once started on the feeder marked *England* there will be no U turns, no going back. For our present purpose this is perhaps fortunate, but if I take an exclusively English section through world architecture in the last four centuries it is not insularity which makes me adopt this procedure!

In England the duel between the medieval kind of architect and the new Renaissance kind of architecture was fought out in the Tudor period. By the beginning of the 17th century, when classical architecture was fairly well established in France, it could have seemed to an observer that in England the battle had been won for the old way of design, and that a typically Elizabethan compromise had been worked out whereby concessions had been prudently

Montacute, Somerset, England: the garden front.

made to modernity but the essential nature of the English tradition had been preserved. But in 1603 James I came to the throne, perhaps the most academic king we have ever had, and educated moreover under a very hard Scottish master. Once again we see that architecture is flexible to changes in the quality of patronage, sensitive to the ambience in which the architect must work. The free and inspirational manner of Shakespeare and Smithson was replaced by a taste

Wollaton Hall, Nottingham, England: a great Elizabethan mansion.

for latinity, by Ben Jonson and his great rival and collaborator – the two locked together in a love-hate relationship – Inigo Jones. And Inigo Jones owed his position and his training very largely to Lord Arundel and to his travels in Italy.

With the Queen's House, Italian architecture came to England in the relatively pure, and by then very old-fashioned, manner of Palladio, and a fascinating phase in the relationship of history to architectural practice begins.

Out on the fringe of Europe, while the Baroque was developing in Italy, France and Spain, the rules of Alberti were re-asserted. And yet, in all the notes and sketches which Inigo Jones has left us there is, so far as I can discover, no indication that he really understood the fundamental nature of the theories which are exemplified in his architecture. He was not a thinker but a practical architect and his classicism in architecture did not preclude him from making many stage designs which could almost be called Gothic, or romantic in the 18th-century sense. For Inigo Jones, Palladio was a cookery book – a very good one, and his scornful criticisms of Scamozzi reveal his attitude. Scamozzi deviated from authority. For Inigo Jones history is authority and justification, as it had been for Vitruvius.

Palladianism, the architecture introduced by Inigo Jones in the role of a belated evangelist, was interrupted by revolution and restoration, then resumed in the early 18th century. Leaving Wren, Vanbrugh and Hawksmoor aside, for the

47

Classical designs for stage scenery by Inigo Jones (from the Library at Chatsworth, by kind permission of the Duke of Devonshire). It is interesting that the architect who introduced correct classical architecture to Britain was more prolific as a stage designer of scenery and costumes.

48

moment, let us trace this movement to its conclusion. It was reinstated and consolidated by Lord Burlington who set upon it the stamp of his lofty and patrician temperament. He was not essentially an artist like Brunelleschi and though, like Alberti, he was an aristocrat he was not a deep thinker nor really a scholar. He was a man of wide culture, a dilettante and an antique collector. He was indeed the archetypal antique collector, and by the example of his patronage of the past it is arguable that he did immense harm to the practice of art in England. The collector looks upon the art of the past as treasure and by his acquisitiveness gives it an enhanced value as compared with modern art. His interest in history is related to his interest in antiques and his standards of æsthetic judgement are almost inevitably rooted well behind the times, as were Lord Burlington's.

I hope that this will not be taken too unkindly by those who love beautiful old things but it is necessary to understand simply that antiquarianism is quite a different thing from history and from art; and unless a clear distinction is maintained it can be harmful for both. An antiquarian attitude to contemporary art can be crippling unless, possibly, it performs the mental gymnastic of seeing modern works of art as potential antiques. This can be a useful sort of patronage because it is forward-looking, but even so it is dangerous because it can have the effect of encouraging modernity for its own sake, and there is a lot of this happening in our own time.

The Banqueting Hall, Whitehall, London, by Inigo Jones.

I would distinguish the antiquarian – as he was in the 18th century – from the historian, by saying that the antiquarian uses the past as a quarry for things that interest him because of their beauty, quaintness, associations and so on and he uses history as a tool for studying these things; but the historian is interested in what happened and how and why, is interested in the *truth* about the past no matter how unpleasing or otherwise.

I do not want to labour this distinction but I must make it because in architecture, since the 18th century, antiquarianism has so often been substituted or mistaken for history, and this still goes on, sometimes under august auspices.

Lord Burlington's attitude to architecture bore fruit in the publication of Leoni's translations of Alberti and Palladio and in the institution of Palladian architecture, by then 150 years out of date, as the standard for English design. In other words, architecture became, if I may paraphrase Goethe, not frozen music but frozen history.

If we now turn back to Sir Christopher Wren we find a man of towering intellect and great practical acumen. He practised in the 'Latin style', as he called it in a letter, and this is probably the earliest recorded use of the word *style* in relation to architecture (much earlier than the example in the *O.E.D.*). But the architecture of the past, both Gothic and Classical, was for him a quarry of ideas about ways of design. If he had not been a man of essentially scientific temper he might have anticipated Victorian eclecticism, but for Wren the concept of the total building, in plan, function, perspective and structure, was the real stuff of architecture, not the stylistic trimmings.

Wren suggests comparison with Philibert de l'Orme, whose book may have influenced his outlook, but Wren was not a theorist and he was far too busy to write books. Philibert de l'Orme might never have written his if he had not fallen out of favour as a practising architect, and there is some evidence that we owe *De Architectura* to the architectural unsuccessfulness of Vitruvius.

Hawksmoor was also the completely practical architect, and Vanbrugh's flair as a writer certainly did not tend towards æsthetics! As a historian one cannot help feeling a twinge of regret that one of the most virile periods in English architecture produced no æsthetic, no writing about the nature and theory of architecture, because the result was that the 18th century had to subsist architecturally on the outworn theories of the Italian Renaissance. Certainly it produced some pleasing buildings but the art and practice of architecture degenerated.

In the mid-18th century the relationship of architectural history to practice was succinctly stated in the dedication and the preface to *The Antiquities of Athens*:

TO THE KING
May it please Your Majesty To permit us most humbly to lay at Your Majesty's

Above left:
Newcastle upon Tyne, England: the Old Assembly Rooms, 1776, by William Newton.

Below left:
Interior of the Old Assembly Rooms at Newcastle upon Tyne, England. This is a fine late example of Palladian influence and the best surviving assembly room in Britain.

Seaton Delaval, Northumberland, England, by Sir John Vanbrugh.

Left:
The spire of St Mary-le-Bow, London, by Sir Christopher Wren.

feet, an attempt which we have made to illustrate the history of Architecture by delineations from the antiquities of Athens, the most renowned and magnificent City of Greece, and once the most distinguished seat of Genius and Liberty; particularly celebrated for those Arts, which amidst the cares of Government, and the glories of Conquest, Your Majesty deigns to patronise.

PREFACE

The ruined Edifices of Rome have for many years engaged the attention of those who apply themselves to the study of Architecture; and have generally been considered as the Models and Standard of regular and ornamental Building. Many representations of them drawn and engraved by skilful Artists have been published, by which means the Study of the Art has been every where greatly facilitated, and the general practice of it improved and promoted. Insomuch that what is now esteemed the most elegant manner of decorating Buildings, was originally formed, and has been since established on Examples which the Antiquities of Rome have furnished.

But altho' the World is enriched with Collections of this sort already published, we thought it would be a Work not unacceptable to the lovers of Architecture, if we added to those Collections, some Examples drawn from the Antiquities of Greece; and we were confirmed in our opinion by this consideration principally, that as Greece was the Mistress of the Arts, and Rome, in this respect, no more than her disciple, it may be presumed, all the most admired Buildings which adorned that Imperial City, were but imitations of Grecian Originals.

Hence it seemed probable that if accurate Representations of these Originals were published, the World would be enabled to form, not only more extensive, but juster Ideas than have hitherto been obtained, concerning Architecture, and the state in

53

St George's Church, Bloomsbury, London, by Nicholas Hawksmoor.

Newcastle upon Tyne, England: Greek Doric columns of the Moot Hall by William Stokoe, 1812.

which it existed during the best ages of antiquity. It even seemed that a performance of this kind might contribute to the improvement of the Art itself, which at present appears to be founded on too partial and too scanty a system of ancient Examples.

For during those Ages of violence and barbarism, which began with the declension, and continued long after the destruction of the Roman Empire, the beautiful edifices which had been erected in Italy with such great labour and expence, were neglected or destroyed so that, to use a very common expression, it may truly be said, that Architecture lay for Ages buried in its own ruins; and altho' from these Ruins, it has Phoenix-like received a second birth, we may nevertheless conclude, that many of the beauties and elegancies which enhanced its ancient Splendor, are still wanting, and that it has not yet by any means recovered all its former Perfection.

Left:
Belsay House, Northumberland, England: Greek columns in the atrium of a house designed by the amateur architect, Sir Charles Monk, 1810.

Right: St Pancras Church, London.

This Conclusion becomes sufficiently obvious, when we consider that the great Artists, by whose industry this noble Art has been revived, were obliged to shape its present Form, after those Ideas only, which the casual remains of Italy suggested to them.[19]

Here we are looking into the intellectual abyss upon which the architecture of an age of industrialisation was to try to find a foundation. For Stuart and Revett, and for most of those who used their book, history was a way of revealing the authority of antiquity. All Renaissance theory was undercut, including Alberti, to a large extent, by the bland assumption that after all Roman architecture was only the degenerate survival of Greek, and it is not a little amusing to reflect that one of the lovingly engraved examples in the first volume of Stuart and Revett, the Horologium of Andronicus or Tower of the Winds, dates from circa 50 B.C., when Greece had been gathered into the Roman Empire for nearly three-quarters of a century.

Architectural history was in an exceedingly primitive condition in the mid-18th century. It lacked scholarship, it was almost entirely concerned with recovering

Athens, Greece: the Tower of the Winds.

and purveying the original appearance of classical buildings and it was overloaded and perverted by the attitude, which it shared with historians in general, towards the Middle Ages as a twilight period of barbarism. Behind the culture and elegance of 18th-century classical architecture there was an intellectual emptiness.

As in so many ages of apparent or real achievement the *historical* interest lies less in what was built than in the ideas which underlay it. When students of architecture carefully delineated the features of later Georgian architecture, as we did in my own student days, there was no asking what these buildings really meant in the context of history. Only in the last few years has the seminal architecture of that period been taken seriously and still, I suggest, not so much because it was seminal and historically important as because fashion has changed and allows us to admire rococo Gothic.

In tracing the origins of modern historical thought Professor Sir Herbert Butterfield says that:

the recovery and exposition of the Medieval world perhaps still remains as the greatest creative achievement of historical understanding.

The question was raised: whether Gothic architecture, instead of being mere corruption or barbarism, did not possess style in its own right – a style which it would be wrong to condemn merely because it failed to conform to the standards of classical Greece. Here was a movement which in the 1750s and 1760s seems to have progressed further in England than in any other country.[20]

But the architecture of Inveraray or Strawberry Hill is important, not because of its intrinsic merits but because of the ideas which informed it, ideas which were capable of development towards a new æsthetic, whereas the classical manner, based originally upon science, had completely failed to grow and adapt itself to changes in the very bases of scientific thought and had reached a state of stalemate. This is not to say that the Gothic Revival was right and the Greek revival was wrong, which would be reducing architectural history to the level satirised in *1066 and All That*, but it is to say that the Gothic Revival was linked with the rebirth of architectural history. And here I must quote Butterfield again: 'A people that lived without any knowledge of its past – without any serious attempt to organise its memory – would hardly be calculated to make much progress in its civilisation.'

For civilisation we might well substitute the word architecture, for architecture cannot be successfully practised for long without a sense of history, without the sense of direction which history can give, without a concept of what architecture means, and this concept cannot exist outside time and continuity. The history of architecture is concerned with revealing the nature of architecture in a changing environment and within the inevitable polarity of the architect-client relationship.

The first fruit of the new Gothic architecture was the idea of style in architecture which was to be consolidated by Rickman in his *Attempt to Discriminate the Styles of English Architecture*, first published in 1817.[21] Gothic had to be accepted as an *alternative* discipline based upon the past, and in a sense the Gothic Revival is a product of Renaissance ways of thinking. This is demonstrated very forcibly in Rickman's argument that Gothic architecture needs a classi-fication parallel with the classical orders of architecture. The paradox is that Gothic architecture in the Middle Ages was not conceived stylistically at all. It was what we should now, rather imprecisely, call an organic rather than a systematic architecture. Clearly what happened was that bad historical thinking led to a complete misunderstanding of the nature of medieval architecture, and when we consider how much ugly and inept design in the 19th century was based upon this misunderstanding we may well reflect that architects ignore history, or accept bad history, at the peril of their art and profession. I think this is happening at the present time in a different way but possibly with even worse consequences.

Twickenham, England: Strawberry Hill, detail in the gallery.

Leeds, England: St Paul's House, by Thomas Ambler, 1869.

Once the mould of classical dogma had been cracked and it was possible to see Gothic as an alternative style of design, the way was open for other styles. In an age when trade with the East was expanding and fortunes were being made through it, the introduction of oriental styles was appropriate and diverting. Oriental rococo, of the kind which culminated in the Royal Pavilion at Brighton, should not be dismissed as a fashionable freak. It was a symptom of a new awareness that fine architecture had been created right outside the western tradition with no help from Palladio, Alberti or even ancient Rome.

If England had had a powerful academy and school of art, as France did in the 18th century, it is possible that energetic and original minds might have been deployed to bear upon the development of the classical discipline, but under easy-going patronage by men whose taste had been formed out of general impressions derived from pleasurable travel reinforced by browsing in folio volumes in country house libraries, the new situation brought about by the acceptance of styles alternative to classical led to the discovery of a completely new æsthetic. It was sustained both by romanticism and by philosophers, among whom David Hume, in his essay *Of the Standard of Taste* perhaps best expressed the new outlook. Beauty was no longer an inherent quality of things made in the right way, as Alberti had taught, but a relationship between the work of art and the beholder, a relationship in which, according to Hume, the cultivated taste of the beholder was an important component. Sensibility replaced doctrine and artistic judgement was no longer based on law. This was necessary because the law, founded on antique science, was completely out of date. Pope might say:

> Those rules of old discovered, not deviz'd
> Are Nature still but Nature methodiz'd[22]

But science was rapidly changing the old concepts about nature.

Bristol, England: Clifton Suspension Bridge.

The thing which might have happened but did not happen, was any significant attempt to reconsider classical theory in the context of science after the discoveries of Kepler and Newton. Instead of this, a very convenient and logical deduction was made from history. Since there were many kinds of architecture in divers countries where excellence had been achieved, and since, in the end, human judgement was the measure of beauty, then it followed that the study of various styles of architecture would reveal their several qualities. It was to become a matter of dispute whether purity of style was desirable or whether the designer was permitted to assemble the excellent features of many styles into a herbaceous border kind of architecture. In either case the synoptic study of history was at a premium. This had the advantage that all kinds of architecture began to be studied, even the vernacular. The great tradition of English antiquarianism, going back to the 16th century, provided plenty of suitably tuned minds and no little skill in recording. The romantic movement in literature, the English water colour school and even the insulation caused by the long wars with France, all fostered the growth of antiquarian-historical studies, while the trade routes and the zeal of Englishmen for travel and discovery brought in a rich harvest of exotic architectural and decorative trophies.

Meanwhile history itself was changing, and just as architecture in the 18th century had failed to notice the scientific revolution which had happened in the 17th century, so also in the 19th century architectural history lagged behind.

It may be generally agreed that the historical revolution began at the University of Gottingen, which was founded in 1734 under the auspices of the Elector of Hanover who was then King George II of England, and it may be noted in passing that the founder was Baron Münchhausen, cousin of the famous teller of tall tales. The university enjoyed a remarkable degree of academic freedom and built up a great reputation in the fields of law and political science. Against this background a remarkable school of history developed, and its special significance for our present purpose is that the very nature of history was examined in great depth. As a result history began to emerge as a new kind of discipline, a science by which we can approach an understanding of the process of human activities. It was, of course, a slow development. It is by no means complete and not all historians agree about the nature of history, but few if any would dispute the statement that the nature of historical studies has changed profoundly since the 18th century, and it must be said that architectural history took very little notice.

While history was changing from a predominantly literary occupation to a serious pursuit of the truth which may properly be called a science, antiquarianism was developing into archæology. These two tools of thought and understanding, scientific history and archæology, were fashioned in the 19th century, and sharpened in the 20th century. While this was going on architecture had to cope with the industrial revolution, and now it is faced with a social and scientific revolution which is probably even more fundamental and potentially traumatic. With what concept of history, if any, with what sense of structural continuity, of process, do the architects of the present day face this revolution? Or are they adrift in a boat without a compass?

In the 19th century more was written about the history of architecture than ever before. A comprehensive study of it would be overwhelming, rather than rewarding. What does, however, emerge from a limited survey of such writers as Rickman, Britton,[23] Elmes[24] and above all Fergusson, whose *Handbook of Architecture* was published in 1855 and revised ten years later to form his famous *History of Architecture*,[25] is that though they were often·cantankerous and given to quoting other writers mainly to confute them, they were by no means fools and they had some remarkably good ideas. Isolated sentences might well, and sometimes do, appear in the work of modern writers as though they were original thoughts.

On the other hand, some of the ideas are very strange indeed as, for example, Fergusson's belief that sculpture and painting are what he called *phonetic* arts. 'Their business is to express by colour or form ideas that could be – generally have been – expressed by words', and he instances such paintings as Hogarth's Rake's Progress.

Men were trying very hard indeed to grapple with the problem of the nature of

Illustration from Fergusson's History of Ancient and Medieval Architecture, *showing his restoration of the Mausoleum at Halicarnassos.*

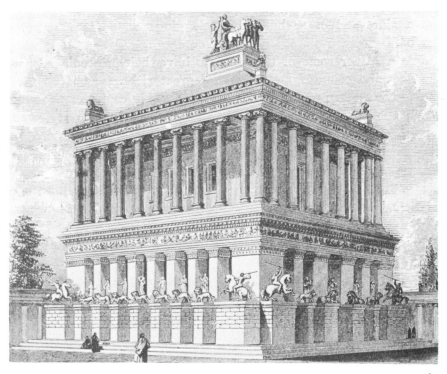

Illustration from Fergusson's History of Ancient and Medieval Architecture, *showing his restoration of the tabernacle at Jerusalem.*

Right:
Granada, Spain: Capilla Real – 'when that ornament is elegant itself and appropriate to the construction'.

architecture, but they never seem to have been able to get outside the concept of modern architecture as expressed by Fergusson and uncritically accepted. This was that modern architecture was the *architecture of styles and revivals which began with the Renaissance.* Furthermore the idea of *ornament* was fundamental to the nature of architecture, and this again is something which it is difficult for us to accept sympathetically. Fergusson went so far as to say that Stonehenge was *structurally* ornamental though wholly without ornament.

It is, however, when ornament is added to this, and when that ornament is elegant itself and appropriate to the construction and to the purposes of the building, that the temple or the cathedral ranks among the highest objects of the art and becomes one of the noblest works of man.
Even without structural decoration, a building may, by mere dint of ornament, become an architectural object, though it is far more difficult to attain good architecture by this means, and in true styles it has seldom been attempted. Still, such a building as the town-hall at Louvain, which if stripped of its ornaments would be little better than a factory, by richness and appropriateness of ornament alone has become a very pleasing specimen of the art. In modern times it is too much the fashion to attempt to produce architectural effects not only without attending to ornamental construction, but often in defiance of, and in concealing that which exists. When this is done, the result must be bad art; but nevertheless it is architecture, however execrable it may be.[26]

Fergusson was born in 1808, took 10 years to make a fortune in Calcutta in the indigo business and retired to London. He was a man of remarkable talents

The prophet Isaiah, a Romanesque sculptured door jamb at Souillac, France.

in many directions and he made a serious attempt to establish a scientific basis for architecture through ethnography. This is very peculiar stuff to read now but the intention was significant even though the execution was unconvincing and quickly overtaken by new scientific discoveries. Long before Fraser, James Fergusson was writing about tree and serpent worship.

What Fergusson tried to do, and largely succeeded in doing, was to write a universal history of architecture. In this he was following the tides of advanced historical thought in his time, and his achievement was quite remarkable. What he did *not* do was get outside the contemporary framework of ideas about architecture. His influence was enormous, both through his own books and still more through Banister Fletcher, whose *History of Architecture on the Comparative Method* was first published in 1896. The obvious difference between the two works is that Fergusson can be read as literature whereas Banister Fletcher is much nearer to being a dictionary. If such a book were to be issued now it would probably be called '*A Digest of the History of Architecture*'. But a more fundamental difference was that Fergusson was writing for the mind, he was striving to understand architecture in a universal way, to grapple with the staggering variety of world architecture over a time span of 5000 years and discover the essential unity; and it should be remembered that much of this was being newly discovered and the illustrations had the impact of news. Fergusson also had a remarkable gift for isolating the relevant, and it is interesting to note that he devoted a whole chapter to Armenian Christian architecture long before its significance was generally recognised.

By comparison Banister Fletcher was degenerate, and in this his book reflects the decline of architectural historical thinking. Climatic, geographical, ethnic and historical causes are cited in tabloid form. There is no challenge to the mind, no weighing of evidence and, by a peculiarly deadly process of illustration, all buildings, of all ages and all sizes, were made to look more or less alike. This was remedied to some extent in later editions by the use of more photographs. The book was meant to be learned rather than studied, and, in England, learned it was by generations of candidates for architectural examinations. Its effects went far beyond the architectural profession because it became the one book on architecture which could be found in every public library.

What Banister Fletcher did was to summarise a century of architectural historical thinking, almost all of which had been coloured by the belief that architecture is distinguishable by styles and that the ornamental character,

The curious phenomenon of style in architecture. Church and vicarage at Dormington, England.

whether structural in Fergusson's sense, or applied as decoration, is what makes it architecture instead of mere building. This view is now so unfashionable, and any re-statement of it would meet with such ridicule and hostility, that even the most dedicated students of Victorian architecture are in some danger of being unable to see 19th-century buildings in terms of the æsthetic principles upon which they were designed.

We need, I think, to recognise the fact that a historian should try to escape from the prejudices of his own period. If he merely sees past architecture in terms of the current æsthetic or fashion he is likely to be a propagandist rather than a historian. He is not even likely to be a good critic. I think it is fair to say that most architects, and people who seriously concern themselves with architecture, are going through a phase of reaction against the Banister Fletcher concept of history and all it stood for in architectural practice. While I think

The Oxford Museum. An exotic attitude to history which, under the influence of Ruskin, brought Venetian Gothic to England. Historically, this is probably more interesting as a phenomenon than as a work of architecture.

this is a good and healthy reaction I must stress that the attitudes it generates are very bad for historical study. Before we consider in any detail how the modern movement can be a screen between ourselves and the truth about architecture let us examine a less provoking subject, the idea of the Renaissance as it came to be understood in the 19th century.

Early in the century the word 'Renaissance' was used sparingly and generally referred to a short period, as indeed was appropriate, and not to a re-birth dragged out for a century or more. Fergusson conceived the Renaissance to be the beginning of modern architecture, and in Gwilt's *Encyclopædia of Archi-*

Todi, Spain: S. M. della Consolazione.

tecture,[27] even as late as the 1891 edition which was revised by Wyatt Papworth, the section on Italian architecture begins thus: 'The commencement of the new era in architecture first dawned in Florence and then soon spread its meridian light over Italy and the rest of Europe. The French have well applied the term *renaissance* to its commencement. It is with us denominated the revival of the arts.' Gwilt was first published in 1842.

This concept is implicit in Lord Acton's planning of the Cambridge Modern History.[28] Volume 1 is entitled *The Renaissance*, Volume 2 *The Reformation*, and Volume 3 *The Wars of Religion*. The aim was defined as 'something distinct from the combined History of all countries – in other words we mean a narrative which is not a mere string of episodes, but displays a continuous development.' It followed that judgement had to be exercised as to what was significant as part of a continuous development, and this inevitably imposed the value judgements of the editors and contributors upon the History.

The Cambridge Modern History volume on the Renaissance dates from 1902, and I think it is true to say that the extension of the meaning of Renaissance to cover a fairly long phase of civilisation is something that has happened mainly in the 20th century. It has largely been an extrapolation from the history of art which is very curious. Admiration for the work of 15th- and 16th-century painters, sculptors and architects has led many people, including some historians, to think that it was a golden age of civilisation and to ignore the religious, social and political turmoil. It has been said, facetiously, that the word Renaissance stands for all that you approve of since the 13th century. It has become a cultural concept linked to the development of humanism, and we may trace this view back to Jacob Burckhardt and his book, *The Culture of the Renaissance in Italy* published in 1860 and available in English translation in 1878. In a sense Burckhardt consolidated a myth and this has been developed by art critics and historians and by the many beautiful art books which have been published in recent years. The idea of the Renaissance, and the culture or civilisation of the Renaissance, colours our attitude to the history of that period – however we define it in time! And why has this happened? One answer may be indicated by the title of Fergusson's book, *History of the Modern Styles of Architecture*, because a need arose to distinguish contemporary styles from so-called *modern* styles which went back to the 15th century! Writing in 1891, Robert Kerr, the editor of Fergusson's third edition, said:

We may admit that the nineteenth century has many sins to answer for, perhaps too many. But let us look at the historical year 1851. Not only does it divide, incidentally, one half of this nineteenth century from the other, but it happens to separate a quite old-fashioned half century from one of an entirely new character – the old half the fag-end of a listless past, the new half the commencement of re-animated future. . . .[And he goes on,] it may be safely asserted that a corresponding evolution of a new feeling for Art has been taking place all over the civilised world.[29]

Robert Kerr was clearly not referring to anything we would recognise as leading to our modern movement but to the popular art and architecture of the late Victorian period.

It was perhaps necessary to cocoon the Renaissance and distinguish the modern. We, in the 20th century, have moved on to a new modern and are in process of making a myth out of the 19th century, a myth which, like the concept of the culture of the Renaissance, conveniently leaves out a great deal of unpalatable material. Perhaps the greatest advantage of reading Victorian books and articles about art and architecture is that they make us aware of the standards by which artists of that period worked and judged success or failure. They are quite different from our own, and incidentally they may give us an insight into how ridiculous some of the things we say may look to a future generation.

The point I want to establish is that concepts condition our way fo thinking about history, and I will conclude this section with another quotation from Professor Sir Herbert Butterfield:

If on the one hand few people realise how many ingredients, how much propaganda, how many prejudices and prepossessions, have gone to the making of the conception of the Renaissance as this has been handed down to us, it is true on the other hand that the history of the way in which it developed – and even the reading of those writers on the period who never used the word Renaissance – is calculated to emancipate us from the tyranny of those superimposed concepts which so often control our historical reconstructions.[30]

If the concept of architectural styles was inhibiting in the field of historical studies, it had a very different effect upon archæology. The 19th-century antiquaries developed a marvellous zeal for pushing back the history of architecture and other arts into the remote past and by their enthusiasm they converted the legends of the Iliad and the Minotaur into solid walls and columns of ancient cities. A necessary tool of the archæologist is the concept or *fact*, as he would call it, of architectural and artistic style. Though creative artists are sometimes uneasy about the validity of style as a means of fixing dates there is no doubt at all that, over a very wide sector of human artifacts, it does work. It is a sobering thought that future archæologists will probably be able to date our architecture and our artifacts to within 25 years on stylistic grounds which we do not ourselves recognise. Perhaps we should!

But the two concepts, of style as a means of diagnosis, and of style as a way of design are very far apart. One relates to the past, the other to the present and future. We are probably quite right to reject stylistic design, including modern-style design, as the basis of an æsthetic, but we should recognise more honestly in the present, what we acknowledge in the past, the wholesome influence of fashion. And in looking at the history of architecture, from early times to the present day, we have to accept the existence of identifiable styles but, at the same time, give due weight to the significance of each, for they are *not* all equally significant and they do *not* all arise from similar causes.

Archæology, being largely free from a practical relationship with modern design has, not surprisingly, made more progress in recent times than architectural history. It has even had an effect upon the way in which architectural history is now studied, but a much stronger influence has been the emergence

71

An architectural feature as a means of dating (a) Cyclopean masonry at Tarragona, Spain (b) Cyclopean masonry at Alatri, Italy (c. B.C. 300?) – but if it were in Greece it would be dated 1000 years earlier.

Beverley Minster, Yorkshire, England: the north side of the nave. The 'typical 12th-century Transitional style' triforium was built in the 14th century! A salutary warning of the danger of dating by style alone.

of art history as an academic discipline. As a branch of art history, architectural history is becoming remote from the practice of modern architecture though some historians try hard to maintain a relationship, especially those few who teach and do their research in schools of architecture.

Brighton, England: architectural reflection of East Indian trade – the Sassoon Mausoleum.

Below: Oxford, England: Keble. College, by William Butterfield.

The problem of the art historian has been well stated by Professor Talbot Rice:

In this age of specialisation, when the mass of literature in every branch of the field of art-history is increasing to almost astronomic proportions, it is hardly possible for a single individual to be an expert in all the fields; for him to be at one time an authority on æsthetics, a connoisseur, a critic of the modern movements, an art-historian who knows intimately the work of every phase from the Palæolithic to Picasso, and a good popular lecturer, is a rarity, if indeed he can be found at all! Inevitably a man must choose to specialise along some particular line and to occupy himself in the main with some particular period. Indeed, specialisation must often be very narrow if the man is to become a master, and one who is concerned with the Italian Renaissance can to-day hardly hope to be an expert in the fullest sense of the word on more than one of the greater schools comprised by that term in a portmanteau sense.[31]

Yet in the same essay he acknowledges the scope for more generalised and speculative studies. As things are now, the scholar is tempted by the great gaps which exist in factual knowledge, and research tends to be concentrated narrowly upon specific subjects. These in turn tend, especially in the field of architecture, to be limited by the scholastic equipment of the graduate in art history, and because he seldom has a working knowledge of medieval Latin or mastery of a foreign language the dispersal of research over the possible range is very patchy with a quite intense concentration on the 18th and 19th centuries in Britain and the United States of America.

The art historian is now established as a professional and the amateur, who flourished in the 19th century is now hardly to be taken seriously; yet there is here a real anomaly. For the student of architecture as such, for the architect who wants to understand more about the nature of his art and for the public which may want to understand the relationship of architecture to society and the relative merits of preservation or redevelopment, the synoptic, the universalised kind of history is important, and it may well be doubted whether the variety of architectural history which emerges as theses, and the books derived from them, is of any help. I would be the last to decry the modern high standards of scholarship in architectural historical studies, but I think it must be recognised that art history is a long way behind other historical studies, and especially so in consideration of its own historiographical problems. Being behind, for the simple reason that it has started late as a serious academic subject, it is still at the stage of building up a sound foundation of factual material, of establishing such fundamental data as who designed what, and when it was built. This process still goes on in all historical studies, though some quarries are almost worked out, but in other fields of history specialised research goes along with more generalised interpretation and is at least tenuously linked with a philosophy of history and a vision of the nature and value of historical studies as such and their relatedness to other subjects.

For the architect in practice, the present condition of architectural history is bewildering. If he agrees that the old procession of styles purveyed by Banister Fletcher is hardly history at all and that many of the implications of this kind of presentation are wrong, he is left with the prospect of a desert studded with occasional lush but inaccessible oases. They are lush because architectural historical scholars have dug very deep to make them so, and they are inaccessible for two reasons. One of these is that the monographs are so thorough and the accepted method of presentation so prolix and such heavy going for the non-specialist reader that he cannot cope with much of it. The other is that there are few if any roads connecting the oases. They are in a desert of shifting sand, and this desert needs replacing by cultivation of a less intensive kind. In other words we need a new way of seeing and studying architectural history as a whole, in broad fields, into which the specialised studies can be fitted.

As Dr Martin Luther King said at Newcastle upon Tyne shortly before his death, 'Human progress does not roll in on the wheels of inevitability.' Effort must be made, and I think that very little effort is currently being made, to achieve a new synoptic and generalised view of architectural history. As a result we have the alarming symptom of architectural history either disappearing from the courses in schools of architecture altogether or being replaced by highly specialised courses which may have some value as academic discipline, but fail to kindle any enthusiasm in the majority of students. It is, of course, arguable that any discipline is good for the soul, but when the effect is to make the student think that the history of his own subject is boring and irrelevant to his thinking about architecture, something has gone badly wrong.

I suggest that what has gone wrong is the attitude to history. Is it a discipline or is it an enlightenment? To study any subject one must proceed with care and integrity and a desire for the truth. This is the essential discipline of *all* academic studies, but the kind of truth we want to find, the nature of the understanding which we wish to achieve, the level at which we need to operate, all need to be carefully thought about. Our present trouble seems to be that most of our work in architectural history is so much on the surface as to be unimportant, or down so deep that our mine misses the stratum of truth and understanding we want to reach, because it goes beneath it.

The compilation of fact is a necessary stage, yet without interpretation it is history at a low level. But the problem of interpretation also presents dangers. The practising architect is liable to lack historical insight and to be too firmly planted amid the flowering weeds of the present situation; but the historian runs the opposite risk of not understanding the essential nature of the subject he studies, namely architecture, though in an academic sense he knows all about it. It is for this reason that the art historian is capable of being, and often is, a very bad critic. It is outside my terms of reference to enlarge upon the principles of criticism. This is fortunate because it is a big and difficult subject! Criticism is not history, though I would think it necessary for any valid critic to have a good knowledge of history, but historical study as such does not qualify a man to be a critic, and specialised study is particularly misleading when applied outside the limits of the specialisation. The great advantage claimed for the discipline of study in depth is that it establishes standards, but it has not been my experience that specialists are reluctant to express dogmatic opinions on subjects outside their speciality!

On the whole I would think it wise for the historian to eschew criticism. In political, social or religious history we do not expect the historian to tell us what is good or bad; we ask him to tell us what happened and to the best of his ability why it happened, what people tried to do and to what extent they succeeded or failed, what people believed and how and why they came to such beliefs and what the consequences were. In art history I think excursions into criticism are unsuitable. We do not, or should not, ask of the historian an evaluation of St Paul's Cathedral or the pre-Raphaelite painters. A good critic or an artist would be worth listening to but the historian as such has no special claim on our attention. His training should foster detachment, non-involvement and not the sympathy and empathy required of the critic. The historian can certainly learn from critics, and they are part of his subject of study, because criticism has affected art, but the critic and the historian are different animals.

History is not only about the remote past: it comes right up to the present day and it is notoriously difficult to be a true historian of the immediate past. This tells us something very interesting about the relationship of the historian to society. His position is not so very different from that of the artist. He does not exist alone and the very nature of history is, as we noted in the first section, that it is about men.

Woburn Walk, London: survival from an age of elegance.

Bristol, England: Princes Buildings, Clifton, belonging to an age when speculative builders had taste. This is a social historical fact of considerable interest.

When the historian is a participant there is a special difficulty about being a historian. Caesar's *Gallic War* is a good example of the problem, and it applies to art and architectural history. It seems to me that the role of the historian, in a contemporary situation, is complementary to that of the artist and the critic. He may do several very useful things. He may show that something like this has happened before, that the problem is not new. He may help to trace the causes, the roots of the present condition. And perhaps most usefully he may draw attention to the framework within which the present is being judged. By this I mean that he may reveal some such pattern of thought as we have already noticed in the present concept of Renaissance civilisation. He will seldom be in a position to say, 'you are right' or 'you are wrong', but he can and should be able to tell you that you are wearing blinkers and what they are doing to your vision, or that you are wearing spectacles and the colour and the optical properties of the lenses. Or he may draw attention to the fact that you are looking the wrong way, or even that you have forgotten to open your eyes, or even more likely that you have deliberately shut them.

In this way I think a historical attitude to the modern movement in architecture could be valuable. The term 'modern movement' is a historical concept, a frame through which we see things and praise or blame. As historians we must know that sooner or later the frame of reference will be taken away and things will look different. If this were to make some of our zealous architect-politicians a little more cautious not much would be lost!

An important contribution which history could make to the development of architecture, in the present strange situation of rapid flux, is that it could apply the healthy corrective of truth. In arguments about modern architecture reference is often made to the past and quite untrue things are said because of ignorance. This is not a healthy kind of argument.

Truth *does matter* and the historian must be concerned with truth. Science is also concerned with truth and deception is totally foreign to its method of working, a fact which is fairly generally recognised, and there is much to be said for stressing the scientific nature of history both in its aims and in its methods. This is particularly so at a time when architecture is again becoming closely linked with science. I say *again* because Alberti based his theories of architecture upon science, as he understood it in the 15th century, but the ways of science and art became separate. It seems improbable that we can profitably look for an æsthetic of the old kind but based on modern science because the old science was based on a *preconception* of order in the universe. It was a very simple man-conceived order and naïve compared with the revelation of the cosmos as we now visualise it. The old order was imposed and finite. The new order is partially revealed and apparently infinite. It is different in nature and hardly susceptible of adaptation to an æsthetic system. Furthermore I doubt if we could again accept the central idea of an Albertian system, which was that beauty is inherent in things which are designed in conformity to law. It is not as simple as this. But a merging of art and science is coming and the new humanism is of necessity linked with theoretical and practical science.

If we agree that architecture is becoming more involved with science, what is the role of architectural history in relation to this new alignment?

Before we attempt an answer it is necessary to distinguish between science and technology. Architecture always has been dependent upon technology, as Vitruvius acknowledged in the 1st century. He also made the important point that technology was only half of architecture and nothing by itself but building. Technology is developing rapidly and many architects think they are 'science-orientated', to use a rather nasty cliché, because they are keeping up with technology. This is what good architects have always done, but they have also selected, sometimes very exclusively, from the technologies available. Seldom if ever has great architecture resulted from pulling out all the stops and making the biggest, most mixed-up noise of which the organ is capable. Great works of art in all media depend upon the subordination of the means to the end, upon restraint of the irrelevant, and this applies to technology.

Marseilles, France: Unité d'Habitation by Le Corbusier. A building based on principles of design closely akin to those propounded by Alberti.

Technology must be subordinate to the mind, and three restraints can be brought to bear upon it. The first is æsthetic, either formal or intuitive. The second is science, which in architecture means distilling the essential truth of function and structure. The third is history, which is about the human context of the building, for a building is not a thing of an instant, like a Roman candle, but an enduring structure for man. The role of history is to humanise technology and this is very important. As an example of the technological solution I would quote the multi-storey re-housing schemes which are only beginning to reveal their social snags. There is little doubt that many of them are slums of the future and less humane than many of the little back-to-backs and bye-law houses which they replaced. The technological answer, so arrogantly propounded by

Le Corbusier and his many followers, ignored the human problems which it was possible to foresee if one saw man historically, and so humanely. Man is not a new phenomenon and there is much to be known about him. The technologist tends to proceed, as he often puts it, from first principles, but as a technologist he has no proper way of verifying his principles. The scientist demands the truth about these principles and to some extent he can give the answers in so far as they involve predictable phenomena. But the historian is the man who has the evidence about people. Perhaps this is an unfamiliar view of history. I do not think it should be. History is the study of the process of human development in the environment where man must live, in the environment which he makes for himself; and the effects of what he creates upon what he is are the proper study of the historian of architecture.

If this is so, what form should the history of architecture take, at least for architects? I think it may be possible to attempt an answer to this question. The wider problem of the future scope of architectural history forms the second part of this volume.

I would suggest that for an architect the important thing is to cultivate a historical way of thinking rather than to acquire a great deal of knowledge of the history of architecture. If we start with the proposition that architecture is the built environment which man has created for himself, its history is obviously a vast subject, and it cannot be considered in isolation from the general history of mankind. This is acknowledged by many historians, as is indicated by the chapters on art and architecture in *The Oxford History of England*, for example. As long ago as the beginning of this century *The Cambridge Modern History*[32] felt it necessary to excuse itself for omitting architecture on the grounds that it was too big a subject to treat with sufficient brevity within the scope of that work.

The expression of power in different ages. Durham, England: in the foreground, Government Offices, in the background the Cathedral and Castle.

Archæology and architectural history provide a great deal of the evidence for political and social history. Architecture could provide much more evidence, enlightenment and understanding if its history were studied more intelligently by architects who have the great advantage, in this field, of knowing architecture from the inside, and therefore have a special contribution to make.

If we add to our proposition that architecture is the built environment, the rider that its quality as architecture derives from man's identifying himself with what he builds, using it as a means of self-expression, taking some kind of pride in it or giving it, for reasons as varied as love of power or love of God, some special character, then it appears to be true, as has often been said, that architecture is the mirror of society. What we may see in the mirror we may very reasonably dislike. The selection, such as we get in the pages of Banister Fletcher,[33] of those buildings which are generally approved and admired, as solely constituting the history of architecture is misleading to say the least. The backs of Georgian houses in Bath or Dublin are just as much a part of history

Houses in New Cavendish Street, London: front and back.

as the sedate façades, and to the architect who thinks historically they are of great interest. They show a concept of architecture which was like a man wearing evening dress, of impeccable black and white at the front, and nothing but rags at the back. This reveals the social conspiracy whereby the gentry never went to the back door and it did not matter what the servants saw. The attitude can

Newcastle upon Tyne, England: the dreariness of modern architecture relieved by the survival of an earlier building.

be traced through to the present day and we may ask whether our policy of rehousing at minimal cost is so very different. It is – we leave out the façades!

I think that history is valuable for the architect if it enables him to think outside the prejudices and pressures of the present day. I think it is most important that he should realise how arbitrary and dangerous some of these prejudices are and he should be able to argue with his inevitable partner, his client, on terms other than his own convictions. To achieve good architecture there must be a dialogue, and I feel that the modern architect is becoming less

Below and opposite, below
The architecture of administration in different periods; (a) the Home Office (originally the Foreign Office) by Gilbert Scott – a building designed 'under the pressures and prejudices of the day' (b) Department of Employment and Productivity Offices at Durham, England.

and less able to sustain his side of it. This is partly because he is less able to see his job in the perspective of history.

How then should architectural history be taught and studied? Firstly we need to establish *levels* of study. We should expect that a general familiarity with the superficial appearance of architecture throughout man's history would be part of a normal non-professional education. Many schools do now teach the history of architecture at the progression-of-styles level and from an essentially 19th-century point of view, but the blame for this lies upon lack of leadership in this field by architects who should know better. It is not unreasonable to expect that any prospective student of architecture will be familiar with the general development of architecture before he starts his professional education. If he is not, he should be able to remedy this by reading and should be required to do so.

At the school of architecture it is necessary to start seeing the history of architecture in quite a new light – from the inside, from the point of view of an

Style used to evoke a sense of history: Inverary Castle, Scotland. The architect's job was not to build a stronghold but to create a required atmosphere.

architect. Thus whereas at school the boy or girl is told that architects did this or that and the reasons why they did it were thus, the architectural student should be encouraged to see the activity of designing in the past as *something he might have been doing himself if he had lived then*. The object of the teacher should be to re-create the situation, the brief, the client, the pressures upon the architect, the technology available at the time. This requires both imagination and scholarship, a marriage which can be very fertile. It also requires that the historian should understand the practice of architecture and it suggests that the profession should encourage its own members to specialise rather than tending to borrow art historians to teach the history of architecture to architects.

It is necessary to believe in something called architecture. This may seem self-evident but in fact there are many people, and some of them are very vocal, who do not believe in architecture. They belong to the death-wishing wing of the profession and are distinguished by their ignorance of architectural history,

'It is necessary to believe in something called architecture.' Vézelay, France: the Madeleine. One of the finest of all Romanesque interiors.

as indeed they must be.

If you believe in architecture, then the study of any architecture in any period can be rewarding. I state this as a fact of experience, and nobody is really entitled to dispute it until he has undertaken historical research of this kind. The aim in an architect's study of architectural history should be to gain a better understanding of architecture. I would not like to be dogmatic about whether this aim will be achieved better by concentration upon short periods of history, or a smaller number of selected examples, or by more generalised studies. One could learn a great deal about being an architect from studying the work and life of Inigo Jones, and it would include an insight into the problem, which many architects have, of artistic fulfilment through another art. Inigo Jones was a costume and stage designer in a manner quite different from his architecture. From the little we know about him biographically and the mass of visual evidence he left in sketches and notes, as well as his architecture, it is possible to build up a picture of the whole man, and an architect needs to be a

The technology of the past is not merely curious – it can be beautiful.

whole man. Being an architect is quite a problem in living and historical study can help the architect, and the student architect, to understand himself and the way of life he is trying to follow. If architectural history were taught humanely in schools of architecture there might be less stress and fewer breakdowns and failures. The great difficulty for an architect without a sense of history is to see himself and what he does in perspective.

Two very important aspects of architectural history are research and travel. History is not just something you read about and learn. The architectural student should experience the excitement of finding out for himself, not necessarily and always from original sources, but sometimes by bringing things already known together and discovering a new relationship. The compilation, sifting and comparison of evidence is excellent mental training for an architect and helps him with planning buildings. It is a good corrective to the technologist's method of plotting parameters because it helps to develop judgement. The more we use computers the more we need judgement so that we can tell the truth to the computer, which is otherwise a dangerously credulous beast. Historical research is a necessary and valuable part of historical study.

Travel is also essential because architecture is bulky and immobile. No photograph can give the *feeling* of it and such buildings as Santa Sophia in Istanbul, which are notable as enclosures of space, must be *felt* as enclosing spaces to be understood. The act of experiencing such an enclosure is a tremendous lesson in design, and I use the word 'tremendous' accurately. Some years ago I had the embarrassing experience in the Borghese Gallery of being with a distinguished art historian who saw a picture for the first time in the original, though he had written and lectured about it many times. He there and then made the confession that almost all he had said about it was wrong and he was very upset indeed. He was a man of feeling and integrity.

With all the pressures there are upon him, the architectural student cannot be expected to carry the study of architectural history very far, and no subject can be sustained by studies at a superficial level. We owe a great debt to architectural historians who are not architects, and I do not think it is possible to combine architectural practice as a career with any great depth of historical scholarship. It is necessary to recognise that the historian of architecture who is an architect may have at least as much as any technologist or management expert, or, for that matter, a practising architect, to contribute to the understanding of architecture by architects themselves and by their clients, and that it is necessary for the health of architecture that there should be architects who can think and write about architecture with authority and with knowledge beyond the limits of the present.

More and more people are becoming interested in the arts and knowledgeable about them. It is necessary for the practising architect that he should at least be a little way ahead of the public in the history of his own subject, but it is much more important that the art of architecture, and I use the word 'art' quite deliberately, should be written about and interpreted to an increasingly aware and critical public by historians who understand the nature of architecture.

There must be architectural historians who have experienced the peculiar discipline of architectural design just as there must be historians of music who can play music; but there are aspects of architectural history, which are valuable both to the architect and to the architect-historian as well as to the furtherance of historical studies in general, and which are better studied by men and women with an art-historical training. I would like to see the scope of their studies widened, as Professor Talbot Rice suggested[34] in an article which I have already quoted. The art historian has an important contribution to make, and is making it, but it would be a very great pity if those who are involved in architecture as a way of life were to fail in their contribution to architectural history. It is a rash assumption that by rejecting the experience of two and a half millennia, and going back to the state when there was no historical thinking about architecture, the practice of architecture would not suffer grievously.

Part Two

The Nature of
Architectural History

IV

History is an idea; it is a way of organising the consideration of human experience which has led to greater understanding of the processes by which we live in civilised communities. It shares with art and science the quality of giving form to unorganised experience. The materials of history are, however, not immediate experience, the data provided by our senses, as is largely the case with art and science, but the records of what men have done in the past. It is true that both art and science can be concerned with such records, as well as with ideas or experience generated within the mind of the artist or scientist, but history is about accomplished events and processes which are complete, or that part of continuing processes which lies in the past. Though there is a margin of history which is concerned with personal experience, as in autobiography, the main body of the subject is the recovery and interpretation of the records of experience. These records may take many forms, such as state papers, letters, chronicles, accounts, contemporary commentaries, biographies and autobiographies, all of which are described as *documentary*. The written word is the main raw material of the historian's trade and he suffers from the grave handicap that many of the most interesting facts of experience and human intercourse are never or hardly ever recorded in words.

Another kind of source material, which is generally thought of as coming within the purview of the archæologist rather than the historian, consists of physical remains of human occupation and activity. The history of early civilisations leans heavily upon such archæological material which includes pot-sherds, beads, weapons, the foundations and sometimes the superstructure of buildings. Where he must use such material, the historian uses it, but there seems to be a clear preference for documentary sources, and, it must be said, that where documents exist, the other kind of evidence, including architecture, seems to be regarded as of less value and is not infrequently neglected.

It has been suggested that history as an academic discipline, a method of organising experience, was derived from the procedure of the Athenian law courts. Like the judge, the historian has to weigh evidence. He has to make judgements. He cannot accept even documentary evidence always at its face value. For example, when Gregory of Tours,[35] an honest chronicler of the 6th century and the principal source for the history of Merovingian France, says of Queen Fredegund that she perverted King Chilperic's judgement and conduct by her witchcraft, we do not need to infer that she was, in fact, a witch who had supernatural powers, nor can we be sure that her influence over the King was as great as Gregory evidently thought it was. We must bear in mind the fact, made clear, we may think, throughout Gregory's work and confirmed from other sources, that Gregory, the Bishop of Tours, had an ardent vested interest in preserving good relations between the 'sacred' institution of the Frankish monarchy and the Catholic Church. His evidence is of a kind which an impartial judge must recognise as being prejudiced. The historian is, ideally, an impartial judge, but like all judges he is limited in knowledge and experience, and it is almost inconceivable that he is without feeling and prejudices of his own.

Source material: a collection of fittings designed and used by C. F. A. Voysey, made by W. B. Reynoldes, 7b Old Town, Clapham, London, England. The presence of these fittings would be strong evidence that a building had been designed by Voysey, but not proof, because occasionally other architects used them with his permission. (By courtesy of Mr John Brandon Jones.)

Every trade and profession is governed and moulded to some extent by internal forces deriving from desire for the respect of fellow workers. Matters which may seem trivial to the layman, if he is aware of them at all, can be crucial to reputation within the profession. Thus, among historians, documentation, the citing of primary rather than secondary sources, footnotes, completeness of bibliography and so on, become essential components in the technique of writing history. The normal reader of a book may complain about excessive annotation but the historian knows that his reputation with historians depends upon his playing the game according to the rules of scholarship. He feels that he must not only be a scholar, but be seen to be a scholar by his peers who will be his harshest judges. There is, however, a danger in this otherwise admirable academic rectitude. The technique, as in art, may become an end in itself. This is well understood by good historians but there is less recognition for the fact that the techniques of historical study have tended to favour documentary evidence. The formidable apparatus of citation is so overwhelmingly literary that when, for example, a work of art is brought into evidence, it is considered more appropriate to quote what someone has *said* about it than to reproduce the artifact itself as part of the argument.

The difficulty of using works of art as historical evidence stems from the fact that any assessment or judgement of the picture, building or whatever it may be, is recognisably subjective, so one tends to prefer the opinion of an 'art expert' which may have been given in a quite different context. It would be inappropriate to elaborate this argument here; the point I want to make is that the rules of evidence in historical study have tended – to put it no more strongly – to exclude evidence which speaks to the emotions rather than to the intellect. (This is the way one has to put it, though it may be doubted whether a hard distinction can properly be made between emotion and intellect.) And yet it must be admitted that a great deal of documentary evidence is coloured by emotion and has to be judged as such. Account books are generally honestly factual but despatches may have been tortuously and emotionally motivated. The state of mind of the writer of a letter – due perhaps to a quarrel with his wife, a hangover or some other undocumented factor – may be a very important influence upon the course of events and the historian is entitled, indeed he must, to some extent speculate about motivation. He is, inevitably an *interpreter* of evidence, an honest judge rather than a purveyor of fact. He is concerned to find out the truth rather than to present the appearance of what happened.

The preponderantly literary and documentary techniques of modern historical scholarship have had two interesting and contrary effects upon the history of art and architecture. One is that similar technical limitations of admissible evidence have been imposed upon the study of art history so that documentation about art and artists has become more important than the evidence of the works of art themselves. The other, consequential effect, is that much of what artifacts of all kinds, from Michelangelo sculpture to vernacular architecture, could tell us about history has been neglected or distorted by seeing it, so to speak, through documentary spectacles. It has not been easy to make a proper distinction between art-appreciation or criticism on the one side and art history on the other. Generally art critics have welcomed the contribution of the historians; it is obviously advantageous to have documentary evidence about the date or authorship of an artifact. There is no longer any point in discussing a design as Vanbrugh's work if Dr Kerry Downes[36] has produced substantial evidence that Hawksmoor did it. But art historians have found it more difficult to accept the evidence of critics and artists as valid historical material and the evidence of the

Cottages at Rockingham, England, and at Auchtermuchty, Scotland. An interesting indication of the way in which the same problem, solved with the same materials, produces a different result in a different place. In other words, architecture expresses people and culture as well as function.

95

works of art themselves, speaking across the years to the historian, remains imponderable and largely neglected. The reason for this lies in the fact that art history and architectural history are still in their infancy. We have already considered the way in which architectural history was related to, and conditioned by, practice, and we have touched, in Part One, upon the emergence of the new discipline of art history. The next stage is to ponder the possible extension and development of architectural historical studies as a part of art history, and the relationship between art historical studies as such, and to historical studies as a whole.

Religious architecture in its most modest manifestation. Friends' Meeting House at Whelpo, Cumberland, England. Each of these buildings is a social document.

Left:
Secular architecture at its most imposing. The Castle of the Counts of Flanders at Ghent, Belgium, 1180.

97

V

The basis of any just judgement must be knowledge of the true facts insofar as they can be ascertained. Seldom in historical studies, as in law, can the whole truth be known. The common form of oath, to 'tell the whole truth', is an undertaking to do the impossible. One can only tell the truth as one sees it and it is a common experience in courts of law that honest witnesses can contradict each other. Bearing this in mind one recognises, as a condition of historical study, that complete certainty of the truth about long-past events is practically unattainable.

Until recently it may have seemed that history suffered in this respect as compared with science, because science appeared, to many people, including scientists, to be concerned with immutable and final truths. This view of science is no longer acceptable: probability, judgements based upon the accumulation of evidence and recognition that there are physical limits to the possibility of cognition have now brought historical and scientific attitudes nearer together. There is even less excuse than there used to be for dogmatism.

However, the first aim of the historian must be to accumulate all the available evidence, factual or circumstantial. An example of factual evidence is the entry of a birth in a parish register (unless possibly there is evidence that it might have been interpolated or otherwise faked, which can happen; such a case would constitute a conflict between documentary and circumstantial evidence, in which case it would be unwise to regard it as anything but circumstantial). The documentary evidence that Sir Christopher Wren was in Paris in 1665 could be regarded as an acceptable fact, but it would be circumstantial evidence that he saw the Pont Neuf. If a detail similar to one on the Pont Neuf appeared in a

Paris, France: the Pont Neuf.

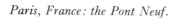

Wren church in London, rebuilt after the fire of 1666, this would be added circumstantial evidence that Wren saw the Pont Neuf, but the *fact* of the detail on the bridge in Paris resembling the detail on the church in London would not be factual evidence of a connection between them, partly because Wren's having seen the bridge at all depends upon circumstantial evidence.

It is necessary to stress this point because in architectural history a good deal of evidence is treated as being factual which in a court of law would only be regarded as circumstantial, whereas in architectural history not a little genuinely circumstantial evidence is neglected, or played down, because it cannot be documented as factual. (I am indebted to Judge Lyall Wilkes, himself an architectural historian, for pointing out to me the discrepancy between legal and art-historical evaluation of evidence.)

Rome, Italy: the Victor Emmanuel Monument (completed 1911), architect G. Sacconi. A building which has been much derided but which cannot be ignored. Historically, it should be studied in the context in which it was built. Under Victor Emmanuel, 1500 years of aspiration had been consummated and Rome again became the capital of a united Italy. This was the architectural expression, not necessarily of the whole Italian people, but of the consensus of feeling and economic power. Significantly, the memorial is to the King, not to Garibaldi or any of the other people who elevated him. It turns its back on the heart of ancient Rome and looks to the North.

In the present state of architectural history there is, rightly, an emphasis upon getting the basic facts right. We have a lot of leeway to make up as compared with other branches of history, where there is a corpus of published material such as Parliamentary or State-Papers, or the *Patrologia Latina*. Much valuable work is being done in the discovery of architects' drawings, accounts, letters and other documents relating to buildings. Such research as has been done by Dr Peter Smith[37] on François Mansart or by Dr Kerry Downes on Hawksmoor contributes significantly to knowledge of the history of architecture and an

99

Newcastle upon Tyne, England: the Civic Centre (completed 1969), George Kenyon, City Architect. The origins of this design are complex and include: reaction against pre-war depression, Dan Smith's vision of a 'Brasilia of the North', an historically-based nostalgia for clothing the tarnished institution of local government in the respectable regalia which it ought to merit, the need for good office conditions, the creativity of the Northern Arts movement, and the aspirations of the city to regional leadership. Disliked by many architects, partly because of its disunity (which seems to be a natural reflection of divided and conflicting motivation), it is admired by many people as a courageous attempt to break with drab functionalism, while others consider it a shocking waste of money. All these factors, and others, are germane to historical *study of the building, and comparisons with Florence, Siena and Stockholm are relevant, irrespective of the evaluation of architectural 'merit' which is a variable. Historically, this is one of the most interesting buildings of the 1960s in England. (Architecturally, I would not mention it in the same breath as anything by Brunelleschi or Aalto, but that is a critical, not an historical, assertion.)*

immense amount remains to be done, so much in fact, that it may be argued that architectural historians should be preoccupied with such research studies for some years to come and that until the facts have been established other forms of historical study will lack sufficient depth to be worthy of serious consideration. On the other hand, the recovery of facts about buildings is not so much history as evidence to be used in historical studies, and here a comparison with archæology is illuminating. The people who excavate ancient buildings in order to discover the facts about them describe themselves as archæologists, not historians (though some of them are also historians), and there is rightness in the term *industrial archæology* for the recovery, compilation, and preservation of the artifacts of industrial history. The distinction between industrial archæology and industrial history is valid and sufficiently clear to be generally understood. But such a distinction in architectural history would hardly be acceptable: it would suggest that 'architectural archæology' by analogy with industrial archæology, was the study of the actual buildings and the use of documentary evidence in the form of plans or accounts as an aid to the study of the buildings themselves. This is not quite what happens: the buildings are not infrequently used as supplementary to the documentation! But if we do take a hint from the problems of not dissimilar studies, it would seem that much of what is usefully being done at the moment is nearer to archæology than to history and that, comparing industrial archæology and history with architectural 'archæology' and history, the truly historical aspect on the architectural side has been neglected.

I do not suggest that we should adopt the term architectural archæology, it would be as unacceptable as social or economic archæology, but it is important

A gin-gan at Prudhoe, Northumberland, England. An architectural feature which owes its shape entirely to its purpose, a horse-driven engine house.

to distinguish between factual foundations and historical superstructure. The foundations are being laid and the next stage will be to build the superstructure of historical understanding. This will be a very difficult task for two main reasons. The first is that architecture, being a complex human activity, is not just a product of the architect. In Part One I have emphasised the importance of the dualism of architect and client, but now we must recognise that even if the

Romantic and nationalistic villa, 1895, near Innsbruck in Austria.

Durham County Offices. This astonishing building has been described as having 'every gimmick in the game'. Built by an entrenched Socialist administration, it seems to represent the design standards of the surburban 'semi' raised to a monumental scale. As a social phenomenon, it is profoundly interesting, though it is extremely unlikely that it will command the interest of architectural historians purely as architecture.

architect were a simple entity with no social background, which he is not, the 'client' is a very complex phenomenon indeed and to understand how and why he is in a position to build and why he wants to build in a particular way we have to study him in his social, political, cultural and economic settings. It may well be argued that no one man can possibly do this, and certainly the equipment and training of the modern architectural historical research worker is inadequate if not unsuitable, but in other branches of historical study this challenge is accepted and we shall have to come to terms with it in art and architectural history if we are to proceed beyond the present condition wherein there is some ground for the suspicion that art and architectural history are not really history as understood by historians.

The other main difficulty of architectural history is that the most obvious and incontrovertible *fact* in any architectural historical study is the actual buildings. In other forms of history students are less troubled by the physical presence of what they are studying. Queen Elizabeth I is not looking over their shoulder. Cranmer was executed once and for all in 1556 but the Martyr's Memorial is, for the architectural student, an actual presence in Oxford now. This is an advantage, an embarrassment and a distinct difference from most other forms of history.

The nature of the difficulty is illustrated by consideration of the contrary case where we are studying a building, such as Northumberland House in London, which has now disappeared. Canaletto's splendid painting of it can be ignored,

for this purpose, as a work of art and constitutes valuable documentary evidence about the building. Nobody will ever be able to see the real building and have his own direct responses to its architecture. This actuality of the building which is the subject of historical study requires that we should have techniques of studying existing buildings, and this implies competence in architecture, in knowledge of the actual technique of building, or so it would seem to me, and we have not gone very far in developing ways of studying the actual fabric historically as distinct from critically. It would appear that we have to develop a fusion of critical appreciation and scholarship, and this applies, of course, throughout the discipline of art-historical studies. We cannot ignore the actual artifact!

Here I have tried to isolate a problem without indicating the means of solving it. The first thing is to state the problem: the working out can then be attempted but it will take time and the efforts of many people.

The implication of the preceding paragraphs would seem to be that, as in other branches of historical study, so in architectural history, there will have to be team work and specialisations, but I do not think that the present divisions of specialisation, mainly by period and location within the field of establishing the facts about the design and erection of a building (date, architect, client, etc.) will continue to be acceptable and I suggest that in future the architectural historian will have to know more history, particularly social and economic history. Concurrently there will need to be more architects with historical understanding and knowledge to evaluate the evidence of the actual buildings, because one of the conspicuous areas of error in current architectural history is where scholars with no practical architectural knowledge make architectural judgements based upon that lack of knowledge. (It is symptomatic of our condition that 'in the trade' so to speak, it is much more serious to make a mistake in the citation of documentary evidence than to make a gross error in relation to the actual structure of a building – such as mistaking a tension member in a roof for a compression member.)

Nobody can know everything and the whole truth is unattainable. It would seem to me, that in architectural history we shall need to bring to bear upon the subject more minds with different training and qualities and the distinction between architectural history and history will become blurred. It should be a two-way traffic because, for example, the social historian who can say something about why a certain building was built can also learn about the society for which it was built from the architectural historian's study of the building itself. It is a measure of how much is still to be done in developing the techniques of architectural (and art) history that buildings are inadequately used as source material by other kinds of historian and when they are used the evidence is often misunderstood, to the detriment of history. If any justification were needed for the study of architectural history it could be that the evidence for many other forms of historical study is incomplete without the study of architectural evidence at a comparable level of scholarship.

Oxford, England: the Martyr's Memorial.

Rotterdam, Holland, the old and the new. The historic event of destruction gives a special significance to what survived.

Left
Liverpool, England: St Michael in the Hamlet, by Rickman, the inventor of the styles of Gothic architecture. Here he translated the whole idiom into iron! An interesting example of the way in which historical precedent dominated the thinking of 19th-century designers.

VI

We have seen that the study of architectural history has been related to, and conditioned by practice until recent times. So long as historical study of architecture was a means by which an architect learned the technique of his trade there was little chance of its developing as an academic discipline in its own right. The use of history as a technical aid to design culminated in the 19th century and the modern movement, by rejecting historical precedents for design, has created a different and much more propitious climate for historical study of architecture. But this is not the end of the old kind of relationship between architectural history and practice. The modern movement is growing old, becoming conscious of its *own* history and learning to place itself in history. In this sense it is no longer proper to call it 'modern movement' and architects are currently thinking towards new forms which will almost inevitably involve the rejection of some of the principles which have been held sacred. I think it would be surprising to any historian if, after more than half a century of 'modern' architecture there were not a change of emphasis, a shift in fashion, a certain amount of rethinking and re-evaluation. To have said this a few years ago would have been heresy but now there is a widespread uneasiness about the *poverty* of the current idiom and the kind of swing which took place, through Mannerism to Baroque, is not impossible. And if it is objected that we have abandoned the classical æsthetic for ever (which may or may not be true), we have only to turn to Gothic architecture and see in its record the progress of inevitable change. Man is, as I have said elsewhere[38] an 'ameliorating animal'. The need for change is fundamental to his nature and his will to improve has been the means of his creating civilised societies. As we all know the pursuit of amelioration has its pitfalls, but man persists and must change.

Part of the mechanism of change in ideas and ideals is, as we saw in Section One, the study of history, the idea of history as a way of thinking about the human condition; and as soon as we begin to think of the 'modern movement' historically we place it in the past-to-future continuum. There is a profound distinction between thinking contemporaneously and thinking historically. In one sense all events of which we can be aware pass into history the moment we are aware of their having taken place, and yet we do not necessarily think like that about them. Breakfast is not a matter of history but an early part of today's experience. It was thus with the modern movement when we were all wrapped up in it, but now we have changed and are beginning to see it historically, just as we see the Victorian period. This, in a sense, is the end of it.

Thus it is possible to see a new relationship between history and practice in the process of being aware of the background of architectural experience against which we work, and although one might be tempted to welcome this new sense of history there are disadvantages. These are most evident in painting and sculpture where the modern artist is terribly tempted to look over his shoulder, to see himself, while he actually works at creation, as being in an historical context. This can make him neurotically sensitive to the accusation of not being 'with it', of being a step behind the march of history, of lacking in originality.

Glasgow College of Art, by C. R. Mackintosh. The conscious rejection of historical precedent.

Thus originality as the expression of one's own personality (which is a fashionable cult) becomes an obsession to the artist himself, and this is self-destructive.

Man is equipped with a very remarkable brain which is capable of awareness at many levels and one of these is the historical level. It is valuable but it must not be short-circuited into other levels of experience. We have come from a pre-

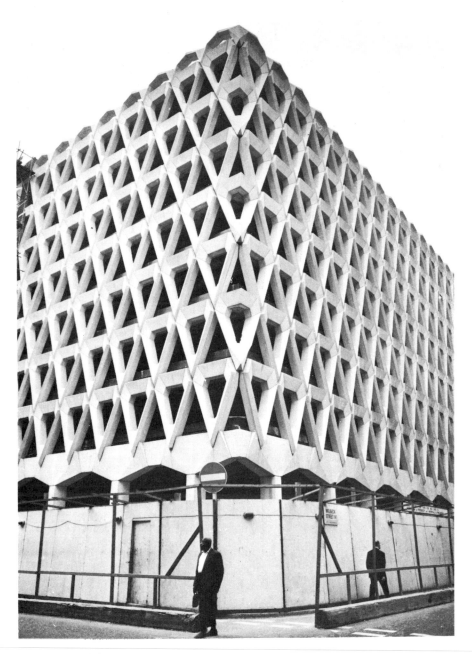

Garage in Welbeck Street, London, by Michael R. Blampied. An evocation of an architecture which rejected precedent; in the present context this raises a question. If this is the way ahead, Gropius and Functionalism will appear in history as a digression and Art Nouveau will be the fountain-head of 20th-century architecture. It is too soon to know.

Ypres, Belgium: the Cloth Hall, destroyed in World War I; this historic symbol was lovingly rebuilt.

Herodotean period when there was no real sense of history, when this level of thinking had not been evolved. This period was characterised, architecturally and in other arts, by slow and reluctant change. With the intervention of historical thinking a long era of successive change in architecture led to the curious *impasse* of 19th century eclecticism and then the rejection of history as an element in architectural design. But what we threw out of the front window has come in again at the back and I think an historian has to warn the practising artist against the dangers of using history wrongly.

In saying this I do not wish to belittle history, only to warn of its wrong use. There are many right uses and the conclusion of this book has been that many aspects of architectural history remain to be studied; and I would suggest that if we were to develop such studies as the social and economic history of art and architecture, beyond the present primitive standards, we could do a lot to correct the imbalance which results in the current practice of the arts from knowing the kind of art history which is at present available. I start with the belief that art, including, of course, architecture, is an essential ingredient in a satisfactory mode of life. We are passing, with considerable help from psychologists, into a state of consciousness about our 'selves' which is unprecedented. Many people accept that in some mysterious way art is enormously beneficial, but its relationship to our total experience, its dimensions within our personality and its potentiality in the evolution of our society remain obscure. It would be rash to suggest that the study of art history is going to solve all the problems but we are only at the threshold of what might be understood about the arts.

Rye, England: the Mermaid Inn, archetype of the English 'pub'. An ancient tradition carefully and lovingly maintained. This modern attitude to the architectural past is an historical fact of our own age. The interest of the vernacular is not only the architectural forms, but the way it expresses the essence of a way of life. Respect for this way of life is not necessarily sentimentality.

Right:
In the Alhambra, Granada, Spain. A kind of architecture classified by Banister Fletcher as 'non-historical'. This indicates an exclusive concept of history.

Nôtre Dame de Royan, France, architect Guillaume Gillet, 1958. A modern evocation of the spirit of the Gothic era.

I had thought at one time that this book would end with an indication of lines upon which architectural historical studies might proceed, but any attempt to define in advance what our exploration may reveal would, I think, be unwise. I hope we shall see a wide expansion of the study of architectural history, as a part of art history, and that it will tend away from the present, but necessary labours of compilation, towards the application of the idea of history to the whole human phenomenon of artistic activity.

It may be easy to assent in principle to the idea of studying art history, including the history of architecture in relation to social history, but the effect

Modern Rotterdam, Holland, rebuilt after the war, in what has become a modern vernacular. A pleasing environment without architectural distinction.

Right: Splendid vernacular architecture of Bruges, Belgium.

would be to change the character of art history as a discipline because we should have to concern ourselves not only with 'good art' but with *all* art. And this simple-seeming statement points to the profound weakness of current art-historical studies. They are directed towards what is approved, what is regarded, by present standards of æsthetic judgement, as good art. In other words, there is a concentration upon the kind of art which we put in national galleries, on the works of the 'great masters'. It is as though a political historian were to limit his studies to political systems of which he approved to the exclusion of all others.

No kind of history is entirely proof against prejudice because judgements have to be made and they are coloured by the opinions and feelings of the historian. The climate of the period in which he works inevitably affects the way in which an historian writes but this is different from what is happening in art history.

116

Here again we are made to realise that art history is still very young and we may compare it with the condition of general history at the stage when there was an overwhelming concern with battles and dynastic politics. These were the subjects which interested the history-reading clientele and that method of historical study 'had far-reaching effects upon government and upon political and social opinion. The rise of social history involved awareness of sweated labour, industrial housing, the social effects of the penal system and other distasteful subjects. From his privileged position of hindsighted wisdom among the kings, cardinals and commanders, the historian had to descend to the slums and mix with the poor. From his confidential awareness of the motivation of Popes and Prime Ministers he had to turn to the manœuvring of merchants, the failure of crops and the effects of unemployment.

Naturally there was resistance, and just as naturally the art historian will be reluctant to quit his cultured enclave among the wealthy patrons and the great artists; but this exodus, this extension of art-historical studies, is necessary and, I think, inevitable.

The great disadvantage of current art historical attitudes is that great art is cut off from its roots. Just as the concentration upon political and military history cut them off from the ordinary people who bore the brunt of the mistakes which stem from ignorance or distorted knowledge, so art history, as we know it, tends to isolate art from people, to confine it in galleries and to certain prestige buildings, instead of it being part of the fabric of life.

The history of architecture, as of any other art, must not be confined to masterpieces, nor is it primarily concerned with æsthetic evaluations which, in

Farm buildings at Yeovil, Somerset, England.

any case, are bound to fluctuate from time to time. The subject is much bigger and comprises all that man has done and is doing by means of building to shape his environment. It cannot be properly understood without knowing the forces – social, political, economic, ideological – which have influenced building. No artist works in isolation, least of all the architect, and no building exists in isolation. We are concerned with relationships, with the effects of those relationships upon building, and with the effects of the built environment upon people.

A modern adaptation of an excellent traditional way of design near Igls, Austria.

Notes to Sections

1. Banister Fletcher, *A History of Architecture on the Comparative Method*, London, 1896, 17th revised edition, London, Athlone Press, 1961.
2. Alfred and Maurice Croiset, *Manuel d'histoire de la littérature grecque*, Paris, 1901, quoted by Collingwood, see note 3. There is an abridged English edition, published by Macmillan, New York, 1904.
3. R. G. Collingwood, *The Idea of History*, Oxford, Clarendon Press, 1946.
4. J. Fergusson, *A History of Architecture in all Countries*, 3rd edition edited by R. Phené Spiers, London, 1893. The first volume of the 1st edition was published in 1865.
5. Vitruvius, *De Architectura* (c. 28BC); parallel Latin and English texts, translation by F. Granger, London, Loeb Classical Library, 1931: also by M. H. Morgan, Harvard, 1914. Translation of Vitruvius presents many problems and comparison with the Latin text is advisable.
6. Gregory of Tours, *The History of the Franks;* translation by O. M. Dalton, Oxford, Clarendon Press, 1927.
7. Alfred W. Clapham, *English Romanesque Architecture*, Oxford, Clarendon Press, 1930–4; reprinted 1964.
8. D. Knoop and G. P. Jones, *The Medieval Mason*, Manchester, Manchester University Press, 1933.
9. J. Harvey, *English Medieval Architects – a Biographical Dictionary down to 1550*, London, Batsford, 1954; and other works by John Harvey.
10. St Thomas Aquinas, *Summa Theologica* 1.XXXIX.8, 1267-73.
11. Villard d'Honnecourt (Wilors de Honecort) *Facsimile of Sketch Book* (with translations by Robert Willis), London, 1859.
12. Le Corbusier, *Vers une architecture*, Paris, 1927. There is an English translation by F. Etchells, London, Architectural Press, 1931 and 1946.
13. Adrian Stokes, *Art and Science*, London, Faber, 1949.
14. L. B. Alberti, *De Re Aedificatoria*, Florence, 1485. The translation by James Leoni was first published in 1726. There is a reprint combining the 1739 and 1755 editions, published in London by Tiranti, 1955.
15. A. Palladio, *I Quattro Libri dell'architettura*, Venice, 1642. There is an English translation, produced on a much more lavish scale than the original, by Giacomo (James) Leoni, 1715–20, 1721 and in 1742, incorporating notes by Inigo Jones.
16. Philibert de L'Orme, *L'Architecture*, Paris, 1567.
17. Author's translation.
18. Author's translation.
19. James Stuart and Nicholas Revett, *Antiquities of Athens*, Vol. I, 1762; Vol. II, 1787; Vol. III (edited by W. Reveley) 1794; Vol. IV (edited by J. Woods) 1816.
20. Herbert Butterfield, *Man on his Past*, Cambridge, Cambridge University Press, 1955.
21. T. Rickman, *An Attempt to Discriminate the Styles of English Architecture from the Conquest to the Reformation* (etc.), London, 1817.

22. Alexander Pope, *Essay on Criticism*, 1711.
23. J. Britton, *The Architectural Antiquities of Great Britain*, 5 vols., London, 1807–26. John Britton, 1771–1857, was the author of many books on architecture and archaeology.
24. J. Elmes, *Lectures on Architecture*, London, 1821; *A General and Bibliographical Dictionary of the Fine Arts*, London, 1826, and other works.
25. Fergusson, op. cit.
26. Fergusson, op. cit., p. 14.
27. J. Gwilt, *Encyclopædia of Architecture, Historical, Theoretical and Practical*, 3 vols., 1839–42 (many later editions).
28. *The Cambridge Modern History*, Vol. I, Cambridge, Cambridge University Press, 1902 (preface, p. v).
29. J. Fergusson, *History of the Modern Styles of Architecture*, London, 1862. The quotation is from the preface, p. 5, to the 3rd edition, 1891.
30. Butterfield, op. cit.
31. In H. P. R. Finberg (ed.), *Approaches to History*, London, Routledge and Kegan Paul, 1962.
32. *The Cambridge Modern History*, Vol. I, p. vii.
33. Fletcher, op. cit.
34. See note 33.
35. op. cit. (note 4).
36. K. Downes, *Hawksmoor*, London, A. Zwemmer Ltd., 1959; *English Baroque Architecture*, London, A. Zwemmer Ltd., 1966.
37. P. Smith, 'Mansart Studies II: The Val de Grace', *The Burlington Magazine*, Vol. CVI, 1964, *et al*. See also, Exhibition Catalogue, *François Mansart 1666–1966*, London, R.I.B.A., September-October 1966.
38. Bruce Allsopp, *Civilization – the Next Stage*, Newcastle upon Tyne, Oriel Press, 1969.

Index